SACRED GEOGRAPHY OF PURI

SACRED GEOGRAPHY OF PURI

(Structure and Organisation and Cultural Role of A Pilgrim Centre)

Nityananda Patnaik

Publications

KALPAZ PUBLICATIONS

DELHI-110052

Sacred Geography of Puri
(Religion Philosophy)

Rs. 690

ISBN : 81-7835-477-2

Published in 2006 in India by
Kalpaz Publications
C-30, Satyawati Nagar, Delhi-110052
E-mail : kalpaz@hotmail.com

Laser Typesetting at : Master Computer's, Delhi
Printed at : Salasar Imaging System, Delhi

Contents

List of Photographs

Preface

The study of Sacred Geography is an integral part of the larger study on Sacred Complex in Orissa. In fact the study on Sacred Complex began with the study on Organization of Services in the temple of Lingaraj, Bhubaneswar in the year 1958 under the guidance of Late Prof. N.K. Bose then Director of Anthropological Survey of India, Government of India.

The study was switched over to Puri some years later to include Jagannath temple organization and its associated aspects such as Paramount deity (Lord Jagannath) and Paramount Gajapati Kings who are the guardians of Sacred Complex.

In course of time the study of other associated aspects of God-King Nexus such as Monasteries of Puri, Ritual Functionaries, and Service Organization in Jagannath temple, Brahmin Sasan Villages, Pilgrimage and Puri Pilgrim Centre, and Shri Jagannath Temple (Administration) Act, 1952.

The present study, which is published in this book, deals with Puri. It's sacred Geography and Organization and God-King Relationship. Two more aspects namey 1) Feudatory States (Garjhats) and 2) Militia Community and Paik Villages are left to be studied as soon as funds are available. The proposal has been sent to the ICSSR for sanction of funds and as soon as these proposed projects are approved and necessary funds sanctioned the studies on these aspects will be taken up.

The present study on the Sacred Geography covers such items as Sacred Zone of Orissa in general and Puri as a sacred centre in particular, Ancient History of Puri, covering nomencluture of Puri, with particular reference to Sankha Kshetra, Pilgrimage to Puri. Detailed account of Sacred centres located in the Sankha Kshetra and an analytical account of historical Geography with particular reference to the locational significance of different sacred centres.

The objective of the study of the larger project on Sacred Complex in nutshell is as follows.

The research project comprises several themes with points of focus representing different aspects of the study. These aspects are closely related and a dislocation in any of them has severe repercussions throughout the whole nexus. The institutional inter linkage of the Sacred Complex is shown in the chart.

The research project is a study in growing secularizaton of the Sacred Tradition in Orissa. The forces, which bring about secularization in the sacred tradition, are :

(1) Gradual economic impoverishment leading to disintegration of cultural institutions and attenuation and mismanagement of palace and temple rituals (Seba Puja).

(2) Bureaucratization and monetization of ritual services resulting in proxy and sale transactions and irregularity in the performance of ritual services.

(3) Inflationary spiral causing economic diversification in Sebaka Community and deterioration in both quality and quantity of consecrated foods.

(4) Reforms in Land system leading to litigation between tenants and ritual functionaries and impoverishment of sacred institutions.

(5) Government interference in Seba Puja and changing attitude of the public resulting in conflict between Raja-Superintendent and Administrative representatives and changes in people's image of God-king relationship.

To sum up, all these forces have combined to destroy the morals of the Ritual Functionaries, to alienate the Monasteries, Brahman Sasans and Militia community, to weaken the royal power and to disintegrate the Sacred complex. Further, this study has implications for broader inquiries into some of the processes of secularization in modern Hinduism.

Nityananda Patnaik

Acknowledgements

I want to express my deep sense of gratitude to the Indian Council of Social Science Research (ICSSR) for sanction of a research grant to undertake the study on the Sacred Geography of Puri: Structure and Organization and Cultural Role of a Pilgrim Center. It is one of the inter-locking aspects of the major study on the Sacred Complex in Orissa and it is this organization which provided funds earlier to undertake studies on four other aspects of the complex. I owe the Director and other officers of the ICSSR for their cooperation and assistance in taking up these interrelated aspects of the complex.

I am under obligation to Pandit Shri R. K. Bramha a Sanskrit scholar and teacher under whose guidance the field investigation was carried out in the holy city of Puri. Various sacred centers were taken up for the study and the ritual functionaries and others who are associated with the centers were interviewed to collect materials about such sacred centers. Personal observation of the activities, which took place at these centers, were of great help in understanding the importance of these sacred centers in the whole nexus of the sacred complex. Various *silpis* (artists such as Chitrakaras, Stone carvers, Carpenters, Kumbhakars) were interviewed to find out their role in the maintenance of and continuity of different aspects of the Sacred Complex, Mahantas, Saraswatis, Adhikaris and other heads of monasteries were also interviewed to find out their relationship with the sacred centers of Puri town.

My grateful thanks are due to the Administrative Officer and other staff of the SSADRI such as Shri Pradeep Kumar Satapathy, Computer Programmer who computerized the report, Shri Sisir Patra for typing and computerized the drafts of the report and Ms. Nilanjana Patnaik who took pains in editing and proof reading of the report.

I am thankful to the Mama Studio, Puri for supplying the photographs, which are incorporated in the report.

I also wish to record my indebtedness to one and all with whom I discussed matters concerning my research on pilgrimage and pilgrim centers with them. Their cooperation and encouragement will be remembered for all time to come.

Last but not the least I am very grateful to Kalpaz Publications for bringing out this book in time.

Nityananda Patnaik

1

Introduction

Sacred Zone of Orissa and Puri as a Holy City of Orissa Province and Famous City of Pilgrimage

Of all the regions of the earth says an inspired sage in explaining the various places of pilgrimage, "India is the noblest; and of all the countries of India, Utkal (Orissa) boasts the highest renown. From end to end it is one vast region of pilgrimage." Orissa is divided into four great regions of pilgrimage. On the southern side of the river Baitarani rises shrines after shrines of Siva. On leaving the river one enters a town called Jajpur, the headquarter of the region of pilgrimage. To the south-east lies the Sun temple at a place called Konark on the sea shore. To the southwest is the region of pilgrimage dedicated to Siva at the city of temples called Bhubaneswar.

Beyond these places nearly due south, 60 Kms. from Bhubaneswar lies the abode of Vishnu called Lord Jagannath known to every hamlet throughout India. The town of Puri where the temple of Lord Jagannath is present is well known in India and abroad because Puri is a famous city of pilgrimage with hundreds of monasteries of various sects and many other sacred centres. The famous Car festival which is observed every year in the summer month attracts thousands of pilgrims from different parts of the country and the myths and legends which narrate about different aspects of the Jagannath cult has made Puri a world famous pilgrim centre and occupy a prominent place in many ancient puranas and shastras. An account of Puri Pilgrim Centre extracted from the Chapter III from the Asiatic Society dealing with Jagannath is given in Annexure-1. A similar account of sacred characteristics of Puri is given in Chapter-1 of Niladri Mohadaya. The extract of this account is given in Annexure-II.

Location of Puri and Road and Railway Communications and other Geographic Features

Other Geographic Features

The holy city of Puri which is the abode of Lord Jagannath, the God of the Universe is situated (Lat.190 47' 55" N. Long 850 49' 5" E) on the seashore of the Bay of Bengal. The sandy shore of the sea which forms a part of the city stretches from the Chilka lake in the south to the mouth of the Prachy river on the north a distance of over 67 kms. It is broken by a number of ridges, some of which enclose lagoons of salt water. In course of time these lagoons have been converted into habitable areas and arable lands with villages established by people of nearby and far off places.

The town is bounded on the south by the sea, on the west by many villages, and in the east by a Mouza called Balukhanda. The area represented by the sandy shore on which stand most of the Government buildings is officially known as Khasmahal Balukhand.

The town of Puri comprises two distinct portions namely the Civil Section known as the Khasmahal Balukhanda, a sandy tract along the sea and the town section. Various Government offices and Civil and Criminal

Courts, Circuit House, Inspection Bunglows occupy the Khasmahal Balukhand, Governor's House (Raj Bhavan) and some hotels. Behind rows of modern buildings are the cluster of low roofed thatched houses of *Nolias* (Fishermen). Swargadwara is present in the coast. The road called Armstrong road, which runs along the coast ends at Swargadwara. Among the monasteries the Kabirpanthi matha, Emar Matha and Sankaracharya Matha are prominent. Close by is a monument to mark the garve of Haridasa (the well known Muslim follower of Chaitanya).

The town and sacred section proper consists of the temple of Jagannath, which is present in its centre and different streets all around it. The main road of the town called Badadanda is a very wide road used for the journey of Lord Jagannath, Lord Balabhadra and Suvadra during Car festival. It runs from the southern gate (Singhadwara of the temple) up to the Gundicha temple covering a distance of 8326 feet. The streets spread out somewhat in the shape of a fan with Badadanda as the handle. The Sahis are Harachandi Sahi, (with Baseli Sahi) on the west, Gaudabada sahi on the south-west, Bali sahi on the south, Matimandapa sahi with Kalikadevi sahi on the south-east, Dolamandapa sahi with Mochi sahi on the east, Kundheibenta sahi and Haragouri sahi, on the north-east and Markendeswar sahi and Chudanga sahi, on the north. These sahis are crowded with houses, which cluster most thickly round the temple. Maths of different sects with vast estates are located around and near about the temple.

The town owing its existence to the Jagannath temple is naturally composed of priests and persons attached to the temple. There are thousands of priests of the temple and pilgrim guides who roam about throughout India enlisting pilgrims and in return getting commission for so doing. The pilgrim guides are attached to different Pandas and have distributed different regions and exercise monopoly over their respective regions. The immediate attendants called Sebakas or ritual functionaries are divided into thirty-six orders, known as Chhatisa Nijoga who function different types of services in the Jagannath temple on a hereditary basis without any interference.

Another feature of the holy city is the Mathas or Monasteries belonging to different sects performing different ritual services on a hereditary basis. Lodging houses and Dharmasalas are another special feature of this pilgrim town. Pilgrims coming to Puri on festive occasions are accommodated in these houses on payment of a nominal rent There are also a number of Charitable houses chiefly for the shelter of the widows and orphan children. The Raghunadan library is having a good collection of Dharmasastras and Copperplate inscriptions and rare palm-leaf manuscripts in the collection. It is located in the front part of the Emar Math facing the *Badadanda* in front of the Singhadwara of the temple. At Puri there is Yoga Institute called *Yogadananda Ashram* near *Swargadwara* and a *Veda Bavan* where discourses on the Vedas are conducted.

Road and Railway Communications

Puri is connected both by road and railway. By railway and road it is 68 kms., and 59 kms. respectively from Bhubaneswar, the Capital city of Orissa. A recently built road of nearly 60 kms from Puri town to Konark along the seashore makes the journey a pleasant and enjoyable one. The population of Puri town according to the 1991 census is 125199 excluding floating population and pilgrims, which increase population by some thousands during festivities.

2

Ancient History of Puri

Nomenclature of Puri

Puri is the modern name of this holy city. In an article published in *Utkal Prasanga*, July 1996 about the ancient times of Puri, Shri Satyanarayan Rajguru has mentioned that during the 4th Khristabda or long before this time the name and fame of Purusottam Kshetra spread far and wide. In course of time the people of the ancient Purusapur village became known as the inhabitants of Purusottam Kshetra because it was the abode of Lord Purusottam. The Puranas and other old Sanskrit texts refer to it by various names such as Nilachala, Nilagiri, Niladri, Mandirmala Kshetra, Shri Kshetra, and Nilachakra, Kshetra, Dasabatara Kshetra, Bhouma Kshetra, Purusottam kshetra, Purusottam Cuttack, Jagannath Dham and Purusottam Puri. For details about the nomenclature see Orissa District Gazetteers (Appendix VI) compiled by N. Senapati and D.C. Kuanr, 1977. A short note on each of these names is given below:

(1) *Mandirmala Kshetra* : As there are many temples with deities which are worshipped by the Hindus, therefore it is called Multiple temples Kshetra.

(2) *Shri Kshetra or Purusottam Kshetra* : Puri has been the Paramount Kshetra because it has been the abode of Lord Purusottam.

(3) *Nilagiri Kshetra* : The Lord Purusottam or Jagannath resides on a hillock named Nilagiri. Therefore Puri has been known as Nilagiri Kshetra.

(4) *Dasabatara Kshetra* : Lord Purusottam is transformed into 10 Abataras. Therefore, the name of Puri Kshetra has been the Dasabatara Kshetra.

(5) *Bhouma Kshetra* or *Dibya Kshetra* : These terms refer to Lord Purusottam who is the highest deity among heavenly bodies. Therefore, such names have been given to Puri Kshetra.

(6) *Sankha Kshetra (Conch shell Kshetra)* : The Sankha Kshetra extended up to 10 Kroshas and its core area is five Kroshas in extent. According to the *Utkal Khanda* of Skanda Purana the area of the Kshetra was of the order of five kroshas or about sixteen kilometres and its shape was triangular and was like that of a conch shell and therefore the Kshetra is named as Sankha Kshetra. The Kshetra according to the Sanskrit writers extends from the temple of Lokannath on the west to that of Vilveswara on the east and from eternal sea to the Matianadi, a small stream. Out of five Kroshas in extent nearly half of it was submerged under water in the sea and the other part which is above the water looks like a conch shell (Sankha). The murdhani of the Sankha forms the western boundary. The Nilakantha temple, one of the eight Siva is situated at the apex of the Sankha. It is almost at the bank

of the Indradyumna tank. The upper part of the Sankha is submerged under water of the sea. At the naval part lie Rohini Kunda, Akhayabata, and the temple of Lord Jagannath. Ardhasani (Mousima) is located in the middle part of the Sankha. The Nilagiri hills which form part of the Sankha has been the home of Purusottam or Lord Jagannath.

Close to the Nilgiri hills were present such sacred spots as *Kalpa Brukhya*, *Rohini Kunda*, the statue of Batadeb, and Ashram called Sabardipaka, houses of Sabaras, a footpath leading from Sabar settlement to the top of the Nilgiri hills, Narasingh Deb was present under Krusnaguru tree, Nilamadhaba was worshipped at this place before Indradyumna arrived at this place. Some deities like Nilakantha, Nrusimha, Ardhasini, Markendeya tank, Markendeswar Siva temple, Kapalamochana, Jambeswar, (eight Sambhus) were being worshipped here.

Sankha (conch shell) which is one of the four Ayudhas of Vishnu, others being Chakra, (discus), Gada (mace), and Padma (lotus). Puri is known as Sankha Kshetra and Bhubaneswar, Jajpur, and Konark are respectively called *Chakra Kshetra*, *Gada Kshetra* and *Padma Kshetra*.

Certain ancient puranas and Sanskrit texts have given reference to the holy city and Lord Jagannath. The ancient records describing the ancient account of Shri Purusottam Kshetra and sanctification of the temple of Lord Jagannath are mentioned in various copper plates of 4th century A.D. which are referred to by Satyanarayana Rajguru in his paper under reference above. Sankaracharya (778-820 A.D. visited Puri in the early part of the 9th century and established one of his four Pithas known as Bhogabardhan or Gobardhan math at Puri. Indrabhuti (8th century A.D.) mentions Jagannath in his *Jnamasiddhi* as an incarnation of Buddha who could be no other than Jagannath of Puri. Since the 9th century A.D. onwards Jagannath and his Kshetra find mention in many literary works. For details refer to Puri Gazetteer by N. Senapati Page 773.

The Oriya version of the paper on "*Shri Purusottam Kshetra's Prachinata and Mandir Pratista*" contributed by Dr. Satyanarayan Rajguru July 1996. Rath Yatra Special of Utkal Prasanga is reproduced below.

According to the above mentioned paper Puri in ancient time was the Ashram of Sages and Sadhus. Very close to this place was a forest called *Daitabana*, which was inhabited by the sages and sadhus. Panchajagny place was a part of the Daitabana. It was the abode of many sages and sadhus. The Brahmins and Baishnavas were worshipping the Purusottam deity at that place. There were no temples anywhere in the area at that time. The Brahmins and Baishnavas constructed a platform (mandap) at Topobana close to the seashore. This Mandap was called *Purusha Mandapa* and there were many such mandapas, it was in such a mandapa that Purusottam deity was worshipped by the Brahmins and the village which was close to the *Purusha mandap* was called *Purusha mandap* village.

The Brahmins of Goutam sect who received gift given by Maharaja Jenmejaya of Soma dynasty migrated from *Purusha mandap* villages situated in Udradesha to Muruganja village. The Bramins of Goutam sect were living with the Brahmins of Kausika sect. This indicated that a festival of Purusottam deity used to be performed at Purusa Mandapa. This Mandapa was situated close to the present Swargadwara. As this Purusa mandap was dilapidated due to lack of regular repairing. Raja Jajati Keshari of Soma dynasty constructed a temple in which he installed the deity called *Nilamadhaba* who was recognized as a four-armed deity of stone representing

Purosottam deity. This temple later on became Nrusinha temple near Muktimandapa. Chodaganga Deb of Ganga dynasty occupied Utkal after defeating the Kings of Soma dynasty and established his Capital at Baranasi Cuttack and ruled Utkal from 1112 A.D. to 1147 A.D. He acquired massive amount of wealth and started construction of present Jagannath temple and earned a name and fame as the constructor of *Bada Deula.* Chodaganga Deb died when the construction was going on and therefore his grand son Maharaja Ananga Bhima Deb-III completed the construction of the temple and consecrated it to install the deities on the Jeweled throne (Ratna Sinhasana) in the year 1226 A.D. to 1230 A.D.

The Sanskrit texts refer to some important sacred places which were located around the Nilagiri hillock but now a days there is no trace of these places. A list of these places is given below:

(1) *Kalpa Brukhya* (*Kalpa* tree)

(2) *Rohini Kunda*

(3) *The deity of *Basudeba*

(4) *An Ashram called *Sabara dipak*

(5) *The Houses of *Sabaras*

(6) *The road leading from Sabara hamlets to the top of Nilagiri hills.

(7) Narasimha Dev (the deity) which was installed at the root of a tree called *Krushna Guru.* Long before the visit of Indradyumna to this place the Nilamadhaba deity was worshipped on the Nilagiri hills.

The deities, which were being worshipped in the kshetra, were *Nilakantha, Nrusimha, Ardhasini,*

Markandeswar, Kapalmochana, Jambeswar, who are all Sivas worshipped in the *kshetra*. A tank called *Markendaya* was also there as a sacred place.

(8) The space from Gundicha temple to Indradyumna tank was called *Nrusimha Kshetra*.

(9) *Mahabedi* (The great platform).

(10) A temple was built at the top of Nilgiri hills for the three deities such as Balabhadra, Subhadra, and Jagannath with Sudarsana.

Lord Jagannath and the Temple

None of the inscriptions refer to the present Jagannath temple, the construction of which probably started after 1135 AD. Therefore the Madala Panji's tradition that an older dilapidated temple was pulled down to build the present one rests on the solid ground. There existed a famous Purusottam temple at Puri during the Somavamsi rule. It was widely known from the time of the middle of the 11th century. It may be noted that according to the tradition the original image of the Jagannath temple at Puri was a stone statue of Nilamadhaba. But in course of time it disappeared and was later substituted by wooden images. The history tells that the stone images were installed during Jajati Kesari in the temple of Ananta Basudeb at Bhubaneswar. Ananta verman Codogangadeva promoted the movement of Vaishnavism and built the Jagannath temple at Puri. The main tower was not completed before he died in 1147. The other parts of the temple were gradually added by his successors.

The Archaeological evidence shows that the Jagannath temple was actually built on a hill, which receded sharply on its western side. Drifting sands and the sediments of continuous settlement have combined to raise the ground at the foot of the hill considerably so that the difference in level to the temple is no longer striking. It can be noticed, however, when approaching the ancient Siva temples which were situated to the west and to the north of the hill, these temples were built on a much lower ground that only the top of their towers reached slightly above the present level of the town. High walls protected the sacred precincts of the temples against the ever rising surrounding. In the Yamesvara temple No. 94 in the sketch of Sankha Kshetra, for example, one has to descent many steps to reach the courtyard of the temple and to enter the dance-hall (*Natamandira*) and the dining-hall (*Bhogamandapa*) which are on the same level. Two steps lower, about 2 ft. below the present courtyard level is the vestibule. The vestibule was a relatively late addition as also in the Jagannath temple and several other temples of Orissa.

The exact geographical location of the temple of Jagannath is Lat 19° 18' 17" and Long 85° 51' 39". It was Chodaganga Deva (1112-1148 AD) who built the present temple. Among the existing temples in Orissa the temple of Jagannath is the highest. The temple is 214 ft 8 inches high from the road level is on a perfect pancharatha plan. In front of the entrance to the eastern gateway there is the beautiful Sun pillar (*Aruna Sthamba*) which originally stood before the sun temple at Konark. It is 25 ft and 2 inches in height 2ft in diametre and 6 ft 3 half inches in circumference. It is a monolithic shaft of chlorite with 16 sides. The temple has two big concentric walls and four gates both in outer and inner walls. The outer wall of the temple which is called *Meghanada Prachira* (665' × 640') and the inner wall known as *Kurma Bedha* (420' × 315') surrounds the temple and minor temples and other structures such a Muktimandapa sacred places. The height of the outer wall varies from 20 ft to 24 ft. Of the four gates the eastern entrance of the outer enclosure is called *Sinhadwara* or the Lions gate. The entrance on the southern, western, and northern sides of the outer enclosure are known as *Aswadwara*, *Vyaghradwara*, and *Hastidwara* respectively. *Navagraha* reliefs are carved on the architecture of all the gates.

God-King Nexus and Sacred Complex

In the 5th Yuga of Swayambhuba Manu Raja Indradymna of solar race was ruling in Jambu Dwipa (India) Malab country. At this time Vishnu appeared in Purusottam in the form of Nilamadhab. Being a staunch devotee of Vishnu, Indradymna had a strong desire to see Vishnu in flesh and blood. One day a Sanyasi informed the Raja that Vishnu was present in Nilakandara near Bhubaneswar. On getting this information one Bidyapati, the son of the Minister of the Raja was sent to locate the Vishnu and collect information about the deity. Bidyapati came to Udra Desa and met a *Sabar* chief Biswabasu by name in a Sabar village near Bhubaneswar. Biswabasu welcomed Bidyapati and took him to his house and entertained him with the highest hospitality and respect. Biswabasu used to give him to eat half-eaten fruits, which were emanating divine smell. Being inquisitive Bidyapati asked Biswabasu where from he was getting such fruits. Biswabasu informed him that the gods of the heaven offered these fruits to Vishnu at Nilakandar who had thrown these fruits half-eaten. He added that this was the daily affair and he used to visit the place and collect these fruits and bring them home for him and for his family members.

Bidyapati requested Biswabasu to take him to Nilakandar and show him *Nilamadhab*. Biswabasu was in a fix, but eventually took him to Nilakandara where they saw the deity. Having found the place Bidyapati did not waste any time and very soon returned to Abanti town and informed the Raja Indradyumna the whereabouts of Vishnu. No sooner Indradyumna got the news than he started for Nilakandar to have Darsan of the Lord. In the meantime what happened was that a disastrous cyclone devasted the place and Nilamadhab had disappeared from Nilakandar. On reaching the place Indradyumna heard a divine voice informing him about the disappearance of the Lord from the spot and asking him to perform Ashwamedha Jajnya so that a *Daru* or a log of wood with divine specifications would come floating after which he would achieve his purpose.

Indradyumna performed *Shahasra Ashwamedha Jajnya* at a place where the Indradyumna tank is located near *Gundichaghar* and on completion of the sacrifice he found that the divine voice had come true. The *Daru* with divine marks came floating and touched the shore at Puri. The log was lifted from water and carried to the place where the sacrifice was performed. An old and unknown carpenter suddenly appeared at the spot and said to the Raja that he would prepare the image within a fixed number of days in a closed room undisturbed. Accordingly the old man with the *Daru* was kept closed in a room and no one disturbed him. Contrary to the promise the room was opened before time and it was found that the Images of Sri Jagannath, Sri Balabhadra, *Debi* Suvadra and Sri Sudarsan were there half done and the carpenter had already disappeared. Indradyumna started the construction of the temple to install the images in it. After the construction was over the Raja went to heaven and brought Brahma and Bhardwaj Rishi down to earth to consecrate the deities and sanctify the temple. As soon as the Images were consecrated Indradyumna made all necessary arrangements for performing Nitis or daily round of worship and all festivals. After everything was over the time had come for Indradyumna to pass away and since then the deities are being worshipped in the present temple at Puri as incarnation of Vishnu.

The mythic account is given in Utkal Khanda and is also mentioned in Madala Panji, the chronicle of events recorded in palm leaf. What the historical account says is that Ananga Bhima Deb had constructed the present temple in the 11th century when he was the king of Kalinga kingdom. But the historical record show that the Rajas of various dynasties prior to this period and after that had donated gold and landed properties and had made elaborate arrangements from time to time for the performance of Sebapuja of the deities. An account of only those Rajas having concern with the deities from the earliest time to the present day and of the main events which took place in administrative matters and ritual services during their reign is given below.

Dynasties of Kings and Relationship with the Temple of Lord Jagannath

Kesari Dynasty

Jajati Kesari (552 AD-598 AD)

The first historical reference of the Lord Jagannath as far back as 4th century when the priests in fear of foreign invasion fled with the Sacred Image to the west of Orissa. Then in the 5th century a pious king Jajati Kesari by name of Kesari dynasty re-established the worship of Jagannath. He ruled between 552 AD. and 598 AD. and installed the images of Sri Balabhadra, Sri Subhadra and Sri Sudarsan in the Ratnasinhasana by the side of Lord Jagannath.

Ganga Dynasty

According to copper-places, Chodaganga Deb (1042 AD-1112 AD) commenced the construction of the present temple and during the reign of Ananga Bhim Deb (1198

AD.-1223 AD.) it was completed. It was stated that the construction was completed in 1205 AD. The administration of the temple was placed in the hands of a Parichha (Supervisor) of Bajpei section of Brahmin caste. Sebakas of various categories were appointed and 36 different Nijogas (service Organizations) were constituted. Payments in gold were given to the Sebakas.

Bhanu Dynasty

Bhanu Dev (1256 AD.-1274 AD), Pratap Narasingh Dev. (1274 AD.-1305 AD), Mali Nrusingh Dev (1305 AD. 1339AD.), Habi Nrusingh Dev (1339AD-1353 AD), Pruthi Vanu Dev (1353 AD to 1384 AD), Pratap Vanu Dev (1384 AD-1405 AD), and Bira Vanu Dev (1405 AD-1435 AD) donated vast landed properties for Amrut monohi of the deities.

Solar Dynasty

Kapilendra Dev (1435 AD-1465 AD)

Kapilendra Dev was the first king of this dynasty who ruled during 1435 AD to 1465 AD. He established Damodarpur and Gopinathpur Brahmin Sasan villages in 1459-1460 AD.

Purusottam Dev (1465 AD-1495 AD)

Several Feudatory States came up and chiefs were appointed in such States. The famous victory over Kanchi was the great historical event, which took place during the period of Purusottam Dev.

Prataprudra Dev (1495 AD-1532 AD)

Hosensaha attacked Orissa in 1509 when the Images were taken away to *Chadaiguha Parbat* in Chilka lake. Chaitanya came to Puri and spread his religion in Orissa. Prataprudra adopted Chaitanya's religious sect.

Mukunda Dev (1551 AD-1568 AD)

The Afgan king of Bengal Suleman Ghazni invaded Orissa and killed Mukunda Dev. Kalapahada invaded Puri and started devastations. The Sebakas carried away the Images to Kujanga. On the way Kalapahada who caught hold of the Images and threw them into fire. One scribe Bisar Mahanty by name who was following Kalapahada collected the brahma (the immortal matter) from the fire and brought back to Puri. Mukunda Dev was the last independent king of Orissa.

Bhoi Dynasty

Ram Chandra Dev (1568 AD-1600 AD)

Ram Chandra Dev was the first king of Bhoi dynasty with its capital at Khurda. During his time new wooden Images were made and the sacred navel was set and the Images were installed on the *Ratna Sinhasana* in the temple on the 17th July 1575 AD. He had a treaty with Mansingh who declared the Raja as Gajapati and placed him at Khurda and made him Superintendent of the Jagannath temple. Raja Ram Chandra Dev established Ram Chandrapur Sasan and during his time Mansing's Rani constructed *Muktimandap* in 1580.

Purusottam Dev (1600 AD-1622 AD)

One Makaram Khan invaded Orissa and in apprehension of trouble the images were removed to Gajapada at the boundary of Banpur and the Raja left Khurda and took shelter at Manatri near Ranpur.

Narasingh Dev (1622 AD-1646 AD)

The Raja established Biranarasinghpur Sasan and divided the Sasans into 4 types: 1) Batchhsa, 2) Nandasa, 3) Bajpei, and 4) Goatriya.

Gangadhar Dev and Balabhadra Dev (1646 AD-1655 AD)

Raja Balabhadra Dev established a Sasan called Balabhadrapur.

Mukunda Dev (1655 AD-1693 AD)

The Raja shifted his capital from Khurda to Rathipur fort. The timbers used in the construction of their cars were brought from Daspalla and not from Banpur. There was rebellion of Paiks (local militia) and a famine broke out.

Dibyasingh Dev (1693 AD-1720 AD)

Akram Khan attacked the temple. The priests took away the deities to some safe place. The disc called Nilachakra was fixed at the top of the temple and a matha called Bada Santha Matha was established.

Hare Krishna Dev (1720 AD-1725 AD)

The Raja established Harekrishnapur Sasan. During his time the temple was white washed and a passage from the kitchen to the Jagamohan was constructed for bringing cooked foods from the kitchen to the temple through it.

Gopinath Dev (1725 AD-1732 AD)

The Raja established a Sasan called Rautarapur Sasan.

Ramchandra Dev (1732 AD-1732 AD)

The history of this time shows that the Raja was forced to marry the daughter of Mussalman General Mursid Kuli Khan. After marriage he stayed at Narsinghpur Garh. As he became an outcaste forfeiting his birth right of entering the temple an Image of the Lord Jagannath called Shri Patitapaban was installed at the entrance of the temple enabling the Raja to have darsan of the deity.

During his time one Taki Khan attacked Puri and in order to save the deities from his depredation the priests removed them to some place of safety in the Chilka Lake.

Bira Kishore Dev (1743 AD-1773 AD)

During his regime landed properties were donated to the temple. Orissa remained under the rule of Marahattas.

Dibyasingh Dev (1773 AD-1791 AD)

During his regime the dancing hall of Konark temple collapsed. The stones were brought from this temple and with these stones the *Bhogmandap* of the Jagannath temple was constructed. The sun pillar (*Aruna Sthamba*) was also shifted from that place and installed at the Lion's gate of the temple at Puri. The steps of the bathing platform (*Snahan bedi*) and *Cangadaghar* (store) were constructed during his time.

Mukunda Dev (1791-1818)

In the first period of his reign Mukunda Dev was under the rule of the Marhattas who kept the management of the temple in their own hands. Being Hindus, the Marhattas elaborated the worship and got the Nitis and ceremonies and festivals properly conducted and made good the deficit due to excess of expenditure over income and this they did till the conquest of Orissa in 1803 by the British. During this period the Raja of Khurda was a tributary of Marhatta Government.

When the province of Cuttack was conquered from the Marhattas the British Government succeeded to all rights as the sovereign power and consequently to the revenue and the management of the temple. Possession of the town and temple was taken on the 18th September 1803 and the officiating priests were assured to continue to do their seba puja as usual. In fact, Lord Welselly had issued the following instructions to General Cambell who was in charge of British troop deputed to Orissa as to how he should deal with the priests of the Jagannath temple.

"On your arrival at Jagannath you will employ every possible precaution to preserve the respect due to the Pagoda. You will assure the Brahmins at the Pagoda that they will not be required to pay any other revenue or tribute to the British Government than that which they been paying to the Marhattas and that they will be protected in the exercise of their religious duties.

On the conquest of Orissa in 1803 the British authorities managed the temple directly for the first few years. A Parichha was kept in charge of the management and in 1805 the Collector was authorized by the Board to receive applications from the Parichha in connection with the administration of the temple.

There are many letters, reports and correspondences in the Board of Revenue, Cuttack relating to the time between 1803 and 1805 when the temple was in direct charge of the Government. One of such records is the report regarding the affairs of the temple sent by C. Grome, Collector, and Puri on the 10th June 1805 to Thomas Fortescue Esqur, Secretary to the Commissioner for the affairs of the Province of Cuttack.

In 1806 the Government decided to get rid of the minute supervision of the temple and by Regulation IV of 1806, the management of the temple was vested in an Assembly of three Pandits nominated by the Collector of Pilgrim Taxes and appointed by the Government.

Brahmin Sasan Settlement

Different Gajapati Kings of Puri established Brahmin Sasan settlements around the temple of Lord Jagannath. These settlements are called Barhmapura. There were 18

Brahmapuras near and around the temple of Lord Jagannath. Among these settlements there were 10 Brahmapuras which were of great sanctity in regard to their sacred Brahminic tradition and culture. These Brahmapuras are:

(1) Bamana Brahmapura

(2) Indra Madhaba Brahmapura

(3) Bhimsen Brahmapura

(4) Labariya Brahmapura

(5) Rathasa Brahmapura

(6) Kasyapa Brahmapura

(7) Gopalpur Brahmapura

(8) Narayani Brahmapura

(9) Bhagabati Brahmapura

(10) Kamapal Brahmapura

700 Brahmin Mahajans each having house site, orchard, tank, land of 735 Batis were donated by the Raja of Puri 20 Goddesses each with five Batis of land were installed in the temples and worshipped by the *Mahajans*. These Brahmapuras are no longer in existence. The details about these Brahmapuras are recorded in documents, which are with the temple scribe. This leads to dig into several literatures to find out to what extent is the temple of Jagannath ancient. The following paragraphs deal with this matter by referring to various sources.

In the undated grant of the Eastern Chalukya King Rajaraja 1 the introductory verse describes Brahma who was born from the lotus which grows from the naval of the great Lord Narayana Purusottam of *Sridhama* or *Srikshetra* which is one of the names of the sacred area of Puri. The inscription belongs to the last decade of Rajaraja's reign, i.e. to the middle of the 11th century.

Management
Shri Jagannath Temple (Administration) Act, 1952 (Orissa Act XIV of 1952)

Preparation of record of rights

As the time passed by the management of the temple went from bad to worse. Besides many other adverse situations the *Raja* of Puri became very neglectful in giving his attention to the management of the temple. Mismanagement of the temple funds and lack of control over the *Sebakas* degenerated the performance of the *nitis* and *sebapuja* of the temple. Economic rivalry and profit motive divested the *Sebakas* of all sense of their ritual duties and mutual cooperation. Strikes and creation of troubles by the *Sebakas* became of common occurrence. The situation was in such a bad shape and awful plight that it was necessary on the part of the Government to initiate legislative measures for exercising effective supervision and control over the administration of the temple.

A bill was introduced in the State legislature in June, 1948 for achieving this objective, but it failed due to constitutional difficulties. The next step in the legislative process was to pass an act (Act XIV of 1952) providing for appointment of a Special Officer to consolidate and prepare a Record-of-Rights and duties of various classes of Sebakas and other persons connected with the Seba Puja of the temple. In pursuance of the Act rules were framed providing for preparation of a plan of the temple and all other temples within its compound for preparing a record of *nitis*, obligatory to conduct throughout the year, record of all the various classes of Sebakas and other persons connected with the *Seba Puja* giving in detail all their rights and duties and lastly a record of all the properties of the temple, movable and immovable including an inventory of articles which are present in the *Ratnabhandar* of the temple. The report prepared by the special officer appointed under the Puri Shri Jagannath Temple (Administration) Act, 1952 were published part by part in extra ordinary Orissa Gazettee of 1954-55.

A statutory committee with the following members was formed. The members who formed the committee are as follows:

1.	Raja of Puri	Chairman
2.	Sri Srinivas Ramanuj Das, Mahant, Emar Math	Member
3.	Sri Rama Chandra Mohapatra, Secretary, Muktimandap Pandit Sabha, Puri	Member
4.	Swami Bichitrananda Das, Advocate, Dagarpara, Cuttack.	Member
5.	Sri Dwarikanath Patjosi Mohapatra, Harachandi Sahi, Puri	Member
6.	Sri Ramesh Chandra Mitra, Retired District Judge, Puri	Member
7.	Dr. Parsuram Mishra, Ex-Vice-Chancellor, Utkal University	Member
8.	Sri Jagatbandhu Mohapatra, Balisahi, Puri	Member
9.	Commissioner of religious endowments, Orissa, Cuttack	Member
10.	Sri Biswanath Padhi, Suar Nijog, Puri	Member
11.	Administrator	Ex officio Member

By the Shri Jagannath Temple (Amendment) Act 1961, the strength of the statutory committee was raised from 11 to 15 and the Collector of the district of Puri became an ex-officio member and vice-chairman of the Committee. In the beginning the Raja of Puri did not attend the meetings of the committee, but later on he was more or less regular in his attendance. For example, there were 22 meetings during the period from the 27th October, 1960 till the 31st March, 1961. In 18 meetings the Raja who was the statutory Chairman of the Committee did not attend and some other member had to be chosen to be the Chairman in the respective meetings. Similarly, in 1961-62 there were in all 26 meetings of which in 8 meetings the statutory Chairman could not attend.

For attending the meetings the members were allowed each a daily allowance of Rs. 10/-in addition to first class T.A. to outside members for journey undertaken by them. However, two members Sri S.R. Das, Mahant, Emar Math and Sri J.B. Mohapatra did not draw any daily allowance for attending any of the meetings from the inception of the Committee till the 31st March, 1963. Their intention was not to draw the allowance from the Sri Jagannath Temple fund.

Shri Ananda Chandra Mohapatra, O.A.S. was the first Administrator and was in office since the 17th November, 1961. He was drawing a salary of Rs. 712/-a month including Rs. 120/-as dearness allowance, and house rent allowance of Rs. 60/-a month. He was succeeded by Sri Laxman Mishra, I.P.S. (Retd.) who was drawing Rs. 800/- a month. In the beginning the staff of his office comprised one office Superintendent, one Accountant, one Cashier-cum-record keeper, one Diarist and despatching clerk, one *Nazir*, one meeting and correspondence clerk, one steno-typist, one orderly for Chairman and two orderlies for administrator. But subsequently as the work became multifarious the temple establishment had to maintain a large staff.

Since its inception the Committee has been holding its office in the building which was all along occupied by the temple office of the hitherto Superintendent of the temple and also bears the signboard "Office" of the Raja Superintendent, Jagannath Temple, Puri.

The Committee had taken charge only of the office with some furniture used by the office staff. But the ex-Raja superintendent did not make over full charge of old records and accounts relating to the property of the temple. Certain rooms in the building were kept under lock and key kept by the Gajapati Raja of Puri up to the year 1969 when Shri Birakishore Dev was pleased to place these rooms in the building with records and furniture therein at the disposal of the administrator. This matter was hanging on since 1960. The records are now being sorted out and indexed by employing necessary staff for the purpose. There was no cash balance or other articles of value in the office on the date of taking over charge. However, the Committee took charge of the temple with all subordinate shrines and other belongings in the temple excepting the Ratnabhandar which has been accorded a special treatment under rule 5 of the Sri Jagannath Temple Rules, 1960.

Out of the three elephants and the establishments connected there with maintained from the temple funds the Ex-superintendent gave to the Committee only one elephant and kept for himself the two other elephants claiming them as his private property. This elephant Jagannath Prashad by name and its Mahunta, are at present being maintained from the Jagannath Temple Fund. During the Committees regime one cow and a calf were received as gifts to Sri Bimala Devi and these were kept in charge of Nidhi Bhoi (a Rath Bhoi) on specific conditions. These were the only livestock in charge of the Committee.

It may be stated that the elephant which came under the management of the Committee died on the 4th June 1965 and with its death the staff (Mahunt and Mento) attached to it was disbanded. The cow and the calf which were donated to Shri Bimala Thakurani were sold away in 1965-66.

As regards immovable properties of Lord Jagannath the Committee took charge of and received revenue from the lands granted by the Government which are known as the *Sataishazari mahal* and the *Ekharajat mahal* and from the donations to the Lord Jagannath such as Bagha, Bhikaripara and lands in the Cuttack Mahal. As regards the properties which are believed to be in almost all other districts in Orissa and other States of the country the Committee requested the Government to furnish the information as already collected by the special officer appointed under the Sri Jagannath Temple (Administration) Act, 1952. Lacking accurate and definite information about the landed properties great difficulties were being experienced in the collection of revenue and also for the payment of Government dues.

3

Pilgrimage to Puri

Puri and its Environs : Its Origin and Lord Jagannath

Puri is known variously as Jagannath Puri, Puri Jagannath, Purushothama, Juganat and currently as *Shri Kshetra*, and *Sankha Kshetra*. Some scholars assert that it is identical with *Dantapura*, the resting place for centuries of the sacred tooth of Buddha. The most ancient name of the place was *Nilachala*, or Blue Hill. An Indian authority says that for centuries past the city has been looked upon as the holiest on the face of the earth and the most appropriate name has been prominently and par excellence, Puri. There is a legend which says that those who were earnest about salvation could easily obtain it by dwelling in the secret of the divinity on the sea-shore. In praise there of the Lord said, "On the northern shore of the sea, to the south of the Mahanadi river there is my favourite abode, Alone it can confer all the blessings which are derivable from all the other sacred places on the earth put together.

Brahma appears to have profited by this advice for we find him next standing by the fountain near Nilachala and while there he beheld a crow taking a sip of its crystal treasure and then plunging into it. Instantly its form changed into the counterpart of Vishnu with four arms carrying the four fold emblems of the conch shell, the discus, the mace, and the lotus. Being impressed with the divine merits of the place resolved to extend its glory. Having already referred to the Blue Hill, the *Kalpa* tree, and the magical fountain it remains to be added that Puri was at one time a forest and in addition to the landmarks above mentioned had on its side an immitable image of Vishnu in Sapphire and that this stone gave its name to the image whence it was called *Nilamani*, or *Nilamadhaba*. This is in short the background of the origin of Puri.

The Legend of the Blue God

Abstracts of it occur in Ain-i-Akbary, Stirling's Cuttack, Hunter's Orissa and other books. The author of the Antiquities of Orissa tells us that a pilgrim of great sanctity having seen Puri in the golden age reported its existence to Indradyumna, a prince of solar Dynasty then reigning at Avanti in the country of Ojein in Malwa. Indradyumna was interested in the pilgrim's story and expressed his desire to proceed to the spot to attain the highest blessings of human existence by beholding the image.

To fulfil his desire *Indradyumna* caused the brother of his high priest, *Vidyapati*, to ascertain the truth of the pilgrim's story. *Vidyapati* accomplished the journey in 3 months and beheld at the foot of the great *Kalpa* tree a number of *Brahmans* each having four hands and bearing the emblems of Vishnu. The chief of this congregation was *Vishwavasu*, a fowler. He alone knew the sacred bower of the Blue God and daily worshipped the image with such simple offerings as he could command. *Vidyapati* asked the fowler to show him the image and after a great deal of hesitation caused no doubt by a tradition to the effect that when *Indradyumna* came, the image would disappear. *Vishwavasu* agreed and took *Vidyapati* to the secret bower of the divinity and loaded him with rich presents including a flower garland from the neck of the image. In due course the messenger returned to his master and reported what he had seen. The king was overwhelmed with emotion and shed tears of joy and resolved to repair to the secret spot, establish his metropolis there and devote the rest of his days to the adoration of the image.

At this stage the renowned sage *Narada*, the mind born son of *Brahma* paid the king a visit and in the course of conversation strengthened his resolve by an elaborate discourse in praise of the Blue God. Immediate preparations were therefore made for the journey. Finally Indradyumna with Narada and his minister proceeded to the Blue Hill at Puri to gratify his long cherished desire of beholding the Divinity-Unfortunately he could not see the Divinity as he had already left that place and gone to *Patala* (underground).

The king saw a dream and was told to sacrifice 1000 horses and eventually when the last offering was poured on the sacred fire news came that a log of wood with insignia of Vishnu has come floating and reached the shore at Puri. As instructed by *Narada* the log was brought to land and 4 images were carved out of the logs. Due to interruption in the middle of the work of the celestial carpenter the images could not be carved in full. That is why the images are unfinished and look like what they are now. The images were eventually consecrated by *Brahma* whom *Indradyumna* brought down from Heaven specially for this purpose. Thus came the Lord of the world to dwell in the holy city of Puri.

This Lord of the World has undergone many harassments and torture in the hands of Non Hindu rulers several times. It is known from the Oriya temple records that in the year 323 A.D. an army of *Yavanas* came to Puri by way of the sea under the leadership of *Raktabahu* or

Red Arm to loot the property and destroy the images. The then ruler of Orissa Prince Subhana Deva unable to cope with the enemy fled from Puri and taking the four sacred images with him buried them under the earth planting a banyan tree over them. From this time until the third quarter of the 5th century the country remained under the Yavanas and the images lay buried under the earth.

In A.D. 474 Yayati Kesari came to Orissa. The important event of his time was the recovery of the images and restoration of the worship of Jagannath. The image was much decayed and disfigured. The Raja repaired the images with requisite materials and clothed them and brought them to Puri. A new temple was built at the site of the old one and the images were enshrined with great pomp. It is during the reign of Anantavarman Codagangadeva that Vishnuism flourished in Orissa and the great temple of Jagannath was built by him.

Robert Dunbar has mentioned in his book on the Temple of Jagannath Puri at page 4 of the book that "the close of the 16th century saw Orissa in the entire possession of the followers of the Prophets and then followed a persecution which has left its mark on the Province to this day. The magic kettle drum of Kalapahar the Afghan conqueror, at the sound of which the ears and feet of the idol would drop off for many miles all round, resounded in the sacred *mandaps* of Jagannath and penetrated his holy of holies. It was at this time that the high priest of Jagannath with other assistants, stole away in a covered cart with three carefully wrapped up images to conceal their hideous treasures in the hills adjacent to the Chilika lake, until a favourable opportunity came for again setting them upon their throne in the temple".

Kalapahar having come to know the hiding place of Jagannath dug him up and carried him off on an elephant to the Ganges. He then collected a large pile of wood and setting fire to it threw the idol on the burning heap, but immediately all his limbs dropped off and he perished miserably. A bysatander observed, this indignity offered to the Lord Jagannath of Orissa. He snatched the image from the flames and threw it into the river. A votary of Jagannath managed to extract the sacred part from the half burnt images and handed it over to the Khandayat of Kujang. The sacred part (Brahma) was subsequently recovered by Ramchandra Dev who assumed the title of Maharaja and in 1580 AD set up in the temple the image with great pomp and solemnity.

After the Muslims were defeated the Marathas ruled Orissa till 1803 and thereafter the British Raj came up and continued their administration until the country won independence in 1947.

Puri during Various Rulers

The Jagannath Temple during Mughal Period

The history of the Mughal rule was the history of destruction of Hindu gods and goddesses, repeated removal of Jagannath to places of safety and plunder of Jagannath temple and property. These destructions started with Kala pahar who reached Puri from Jajpur in the 16th century A.D. During the period from 1568 to 1589 Raja Mansingh set out for the conquest of Orissa and after departure of Mansingh the Afghans defied Mughal authority and desecrated the Jagannath temple. Mansingh again marched to Orissa in the years 1591-92 AD and the situations were such that he favoured Raja Ramchandra Deva stationed at his capital Khurda and nominated him as the custodian of the Jagannath temple. To make the story short Mansingh made Ramchandra Deva the Raja of the kingdom of Orissa. It was during this time one Gouri Mahadei, a consort of Raja Mansingh, built the hall of the Mukti Mandap within the Jagannath temple precincts. The

Jagannath temple became the most famous Hindu temple in the Mughal empire. It was unbelievable that those who plundered the temple and carried off the idols to throw them in the river Ganges or burnt them into ashes changed their mind and looked upon them with the greatest reverence and respect.

But this attitude of respect did not last long. During the reign of Jahangir the Jagannath temple was the target of attack by the Mughal Subadars of Orissa. Orissa was made a *Suba* in 1607 when one Hashim Khan was appointed as a *Subadar* of Orissa. Many a time the deities were carried away to places of safety in order to avoid destruction of the temple by the Mughal chiefs. During the time of Murshid Quli II who became the Deputy Subadar of Orissa in 1734 the deities were brought back to the temple by the priests as permitted by Murshid Quli II because the absence of Jagannath from the temple at Puri caused annually a huge loss of Rs. Nine lakhs which the pilgrims were paying as pilgrim tax. The ordeal of Jagannath was at last over when the Marathas took over Orissa by defeating the Mughal rulers. It was Bira Kishore Deva who was then the Gajapati Raja of Orissa stationed at the Khurda capital. During his rule Raghuji Bhonsle marched towards Cuttack and sent his agent named Bahadur Khan with a letter addressed to the priests of Jagannath not to get *panicky* due to the Maratha raid and continue their services in the Jagannath temple as usual. The Muslim rule in Orissa ended in 1759. With the appointment of Sheo Bhat Sathe as the Subasdar in 1760, Orissa came directly under the control of the Marathas.

The Jagannath Temple during Maratha Period

After the Mughal rule came the Maratha administration. Being Hindus they had a great honour for the Lord Jagannath. During the Maratha rule there was no need to shift Jagannath from the temple to safer places

1. Temple of Lord Jagannath Puri.

2. Gundicha Temple.

3. Car Festival.

4. Entrance Gate of Sri Lokanath Temple.

5. Manikarnika Sahi.

6. Markendaya Sacred Tank.

7. Temple of Goddess Baseli.

8. Alara Nath (Brahmagiri).

9. Baseli Sahi.

10. Temple of Jameswar Mahadev.

11. Temple of Sri Lokanath.

12. Indradyumna Tank.

13. Temple of Markendaya Mahadeva.

14. Grand Road (Bada Danda).

as was done during the Mughal rule. The Maratha rulers were spending annually 20,000 *Kahanas* of cowries or about Rs. 6000 in those days for the charitable purposes in the Jagannath temple. The Maratha government took keen interest in the management of the temple and performance of the daily *nitis* or *sebapuja* of the deities. The Maratha rulers extended help and support to those who were coming on pilgrimage to Puri.

In those days the pilgrims used to come to Puri by the help of elephants, horses, palanquins, boats and most of them came by walking covering long distance from their native place. While walking they had to face many difficulties such as robbery, illness, attack by wild animals. Generally the pilgrims travelled in a group so that they protected themselves and the robbers could not attack them. In spite of these troubles the pilgrims were encouraged to visit Puri because of the care taken by the Maratha Government. Passports (*Dustak*) were issued to the pilgrims without any cumbersome procedures to enter the Puri town and have *darshan* of the deities. The State governments were intimated to issue similar passports to those who intended to come on pilgrimage to Puri

The Government gave special attention for the safety of the pilgrims coming to visit Puri and made necessary arrangements at Puri for the comfort of the visiting pilgrims. The organization of tourism was well developed and was one of the principal functions of the Maratha Government in Orissa. Prof. Pravat Mukherjee has given many instances of persons to whom passports were issued to come on pilgrimage to Puri individually or in a group or with their family members.

The letters show that during the Maratha rule, the road to Puri was not safe. Rich persons like Ram Shankar and Bishannath took with them armed retainers, coolies, horses and carried food materials. The Maratha officers were requested to give them facilities during their journey to Puri.

The Maratha Government was also very liberal in issuing passports even to the Muslims to visit Lord Jagannath at Puri, particularly during car festival when the deities were brought out of the temple and seated in their respective cars drawn from the temple to *Gundicha ghar* along the grand road. This was the time when the public irrespective of caste, creed, nationality got a chance for *darshan* of the deities. The devotees of Lord Jagannath who were forbidden to enter the temple on the grounds of their birth in low caste communities availed themselves of the opportunities to have *darshan* of Jagannath while in car outside the temple during car festival.

In the 18th century there were no convenient route to Puri. People coming from Banaras used to make boat journey in the river Ganges upto Calcutta from where they came walking to Puri. Generally people walked on the banks of the rivers upto certain distance and cover the rest of the distance by walking. During the period of Raja Ram Pandit who was the governor of Orissa the pilgrims coming from distant places like Bombay, Gujarat, Maharastra, were given maximum assistance in Orissa for their comfortable stay at Puri and have *darshan* peacefully. When Sankar and Visvanath came on pilgrimage to Puri nearly 60 people accompanied them. The Government made all necessary arrangements for their stay at Puri comfortably and also for their return journey after having *darshan* of the Lord Jagannath with least difficulties.

During the Maratha rule the temple of Lord Jagannath was managed under the superintendence of the Raja of Khurda and the sources of income were of the revenue collected from *Sataisa Hazari Mahal*, a vast landed property donated by Raghuji Bhonsla of Nagpur. Other sources were town duties, sales tax from businessmen, sale proceeds of *Mahaprasad* and *Kotha Khanja* or assignment of land revenue. Due to mismanagement the income from these sources was not sufficient to meet the expenses of the temple. In such a situation the Maratha Government had to provide additional funds to meet the deficiency.

During the Maratha rule the management of the temple was vested with the *Parichhas*. There were 3 *Parichhas* and among them the first and the third *Parichhas* were the Marathas and the second one was a man of the soil. He was called Jagannath Rajguru. The third one was called *Satais Hazari Mahal Parichha* because he was collecting revenue from the *Satais Hazari Mahal*. The revenue collected was of Rs. 27000 *Kahanas* of cowries.

The *Parichhas* became corrupted and as a result the Government had to pay additional amount to meet the deficiency that occurred in the temple treasury.

In addition to this the Government had to meet the expenditure for the construction of the chariots, which was of the order of 30 to 40 thousand rupees per annum. The Raja of Daspalla used to supply logs of wood free of cost and therefore he was exempted from paying tribute unlike the Rajas of Mayurbhanj, Nilgiri, Khurda who were paying tribute to the Maratha Government.

In order to recompensate the loss that occurred due to the heavy expenditure required for the construction of the Cars the Maratha Government continued the practice of collecting pilgrim tax which was levied since the time of Mughal Government. The *Pratiharis* of the temple used to collect at the rate of six annas per rupee from the pilgrims and the Maratha Government imposed a tax on the *Pratiharis* in order to make up the loss to some extent.

The Jagannath Temple during British Period

The British conquered Orissa and took possession of the Jagannath temple administration in the year 1803. Lord

Welleslley, Governor General intimated to Lieutenant Colonel Lionel Campbell who was despatched to take possession of the province of Cuttack, that he should take utmost care and precaution so that the inhabitants of Orissa should not rebel against the British authority. He wanted to secure the goodwill of the people of Orissa by appealing to their religious sentiment. He was aware of their deep veneration for Jagannath, the temple of which was most celebrated in India.

Campbell was told : "The question of pilgrims who resort to the Jagannath temple from all parts of the country will require your particular attention. You will be careful to afford the pilgrims ample protection and treat them with every mark of consideration and kindness. On your arrival at Jaggernaut (Jagannath) you will employ every precaution to preserve the respect due to the Pagoda and to the religious prejudices of the Brahmins and pilgrims". Campbell was also warned : "The Brahmins are supposed to derive considerable profit from the duties levied from the pilgrims. It will not be therefore possible at the present moment to interrupt the system which prevails in the collection of those duties".

A Board of Commissioners was constituted on 3rd August 1803 to look into the affairs of Cuttack. The Board appointed James Hunter as Collector of Jaggernaut to collect revenue and to superintend the temple affairs. The Commissioners were anxious for smooth celebration of the Car festival to be held for the first time under the British rule in July 1804. On 29 October 1804 Charles Groomes assumed office as the Judge, Magistrate and Collector of the Southern Division. The Board of Commissioners directed Groome to pay Rs. 10,000 to Dol Govinda, the *Rath Parichha* to enable him to construct the Cars (*raths*). The Commissioners wrote to the Secretary to the Government of Bengal seeking his approval of renewing the Toll which was levied on the pilgrims during the Maratha regime. The Governor General wanted a report on the internal administration of the temple before making any legislation for the removal of the pilgrim tax. Groomc was directed by the Board of Commissioners to proceed to Puri and submit a report on the customs regarding levying and collecting taxes from the pilgrims during the Maratha rule.

Grooms in his report recommended imposition of the pilgrim tax after modifying the system of collection that prevailed under the Maratha rule. The Board of Commissioners submitted a draft of a regulation for the management of the temple of Jagannath to the Board of Revenue. They recommended imposition of the pilgrim tax and appointment of a Collector of Pilgrim tax. The Board of Revenue on 17th June, forwarded the draft to the Bengal Government which received the approval of the Governor General in Council.

In July 1805 Harcourt visited Puri to witness the Car festival. He wrote that the pilgrims and the priests appeared to be highly gratified by the attendance of European Gentlemen and received them with shouts and clapping. He also observed that the pilgrims and the priests were highly gratified by the actions taken by the British Government for the feelings of respect and attention to the priests.

On 5 Sept. 1805, Regulation XII of 1805 was passed, making provision for the collection of tax from the pilgrims resorting to the temple of Jagannath.

In November 1805, the Board of Revenue prepared the draft of a Regulation in conformity to the provisions contained in section 31 of Regulation XII of 1805, for the collection of a tax on the pilgrims resorting to the temple of Jagannath. One James Hunter was deputed to officiate as the collector of pilgrim tax. He was appointed on 21 November 1805 on a salary of Rs. 500 per month with a commission of 1 percent of the gross collection of the pilgrim tax. The pilgrim tax was collected from January 1806, and was imposed on 22 January 1806. But on the first day, the pilgrims were allowed to enter Puri without making any payment. Next day five *Bhurrung Jatrees* paid Rs. 2 each. The number of pilgrims considerably increased within a few days. The crowd was so great that it was necessary to station four "*Batpeadas*" (road peons) to control the crowd at *Athuranulla ghat*. Hunter asked the *Pandas* not to take presents from the pilgrims without the knowledge of the Collector of the pilgrim tax. In addition to the pilgrim tax the Pandas were allowed to collect a fee from the pilgrims exclusive of the tax payable to Government.

A Regulation IV was passed on 3rd April 1806 fixing the rate of tax to be paid by the pilgrims. A tax at *Athuranulla ghat* was fixed at 10 rupees and at Lokanath, 6 rupees on each person of the class of pilgrims called '*Laal Jatrees*'. The tax on all other pilgrims was levied at the rate of 2 rupees. The officers attached to the temple were strictly forbidden from making any demands of money exclusive of the tax and the fees specified. The superintendence of the temple of Jagannath and its interior economy, the conduct and management of its officers and the entire control over the priests, officers and servants attached to the idol and to the temple, were vested in an assembly of Pandits or learned Brahmins, who on all occasions, were guided by the recorded rules concerning the institution of the temple and by long established usage.

The government released Mukunda Deva from confinement. He was allowed to stay at Puri and was granted *Malikana* amounting one tenth of the revenue of the Khurda estate from 1808-1809.

George Webb the Collector of Cuttack was asked to bring up the accounts of the receipts and disbursement and to make a full enquiry respecting the lands assigned for the support of the temple. On the 19 December 1807

Webb submitted his repot to the Board of Revenue. The accounts given in his report are as follows:

1.	Average expenses of the Temple of every kind for the last six years (two years of Maratha rule and four years of British rule)	Rs. 65,999-5
2.	Average every receipts during the last six years	Rs. 30,884-0
3.	Cash advanced	Rs. 29,335-11
4.	Aggregate amount proposed sicca	Rs. 56,342-9

According to Groome's Report, the revenue of the Temple at the time of the British conquest was derived from the following sources :

1.	Eleven Mauzas comprising twenty villages in the Satais Hazari Mahals*	Rs. 11,848
2.	Small plots of land	Rs. 157
3.	Khanjahs or fixed monetary assignments in Mogulbundee or British Orissa	Rs. 17,177
4.	*Khanjahs* in rent free lands in Mogulbundee	Rs. 7,262
5.	*Khanjahs* in certain *killas*	Rs. 778
6.	Resources of the Temple under various heads such as poll tax	Rs. 10,638
	Sicca Rupees	Rs. 47,877-7-6

The Board of Revenue asked George Webb, the Collector Cuttack, to suggest rules for regulating the Pilgrim tax. Webb suggested that 'Laal Jatrees, should be allowed access to the temple for 16 days. He also suggested provision for a second class of pilgrims to be called *'Nim*

Laal'. They would be allowed access to the Temple for a week, paying Rs. 5 at Atharanalla and Rs. 3 at Loknath ghat.

The Bhurrangs, paying Rs. 2 at Atharanalla ghat, would have access to the Temple for 4 days, instead of 5 days, as was hitherto allowed. The fourth class, commonly called the *Kangals*, "being pilgrims in actual state of poverty" would have access to the Temple for one day. Webb insisted that the *Nim Laal*, *Bhurrang* and *Kangal* pilgrims must be attended by the Pandas to guide them through the ceremonies. At this juncture the Board of Revenue seriously felt to entrust the Raja of Khurda with the affairs of the temple as soon as possible.

The Governor General asked Charles Buller, who was stationed at Cuttack as settlement commissioner to submit a scheme for collection of tax. Charles Buller, a member of the Board of Revenue, consistently insisted on the appointment of the Raja of Khurda as the superintendent of the Temple. He wrote to the Governor General suggesting that a regulation be immediately enacted for vesting

---

* Satais Hazari Mahals : There were originally five villages-Kapileswarpur, Batgaon, Bir Pratappur, Salejoree, Ootarkona, which were given three hundred years ago by the Rajas of Kurda. Subsequently, Swanlo, Pruohitpur, Alsurrang (Astarang) and Mohuree etc., were granted by other persons. Majority of the villagers were situated in pergunah Rahang.

The revenue of the Satais Hazari Mahals was much less than rupees twenty seven thousand. Groome in his report pointed out that taking advantage of the change in the administration the Matdharis "shamelessly practised embezzlement" and appropriated the lands which were given to them as 'Kothkhanjah' or supply of bhog to the temple.

An endowment of the temple of Jagannath known as Math Rajoo was held by Narain Das, who sold a portion of it to a Muhammadan named Latif Khan, for a small sum. The property known as "Latif Jumma" was sold by the owner after four years to a person named Sivaprasad Singh. Scott Warring Offg. Collector, held all these transactions to be illegal in 1811.

superintendence of the temple of Jagannath in the Raja of Khurda.

The draft of the proposed Regulation was sent to the Court of Directors for confirmation. After deliberating pros and cons of the matter at various levels of the Government it was decided to vest the affair of the temple with the Raja of Khurda. The decisions taken in this matter are stated below.

A regulation for rescinding regulations IV and V of 1806 and for substitution of rules in lieu of those enacted in the said regulations, for levying duties from the pilgrims resorting to Juggernath, and for superintendence and management of the affairs of the Temple was passed by the Governor General in Council on 28 April 1809, (1224 Higree, 1216 Fassili).

It was stated in preamble : "Whereas it has appeared that the rules at present in force for levying duties from the pilgrims and for the superintendence and management of the affairs of the temple of Juggernath have been in some respects attended with difficulty and inconvenience, the Governor General in Council with a view to afford every facility to the different classes of Hindoos in the performance of their religious ceremonies and with a view to the better management of the internal affairs of the Temple" passed the following regulation.

The clauses were : First "The superintendence of the temple of Juggernath and its internal economy and management of the affairs and control over the priests and servants attached to the temple are hereby vested in the Rajah of Khoordah who on all occasions shall be guided by the recorded rules and institutions of the temple or by established usage".

Second "The Rajah of Khoordah and his successors shall have the charge vested in them so long as they shall continue to conduct themselves with integrity, deligence and propriety; but nothing contained in the Regulation shall be constrained to preclude the Governor General in Council from removing the present Rajah or any of his successors on proof of misconduct in such persons made to the satisfaction of the Governor General".

The Third clause is unimportant.

Fourth : "Three *Dewl Purchas* are to be appointed by the Collector of Cuttack subject to the confirmation by the Governor General and they are not to be removed from the office without the sanction of the Governor General".

"In the event of any orders issued by the Rajah being inconsistent with the recorded rules and institutions of the temple or with its ancient and established usages, the Purchas are to represent to the Governor General in Council, if it should appear that the interposition of Government is necessary for the restoration of good order and the prevention of disputes and irregularity."

"The Third *Dewl Purcha* shall execute the duty of the *Sattais Huzzaree Purcha*, and it shall be his duty to give an account to the Collector of the tax of all offerings and presents made to the idol".

Fifth : "A tax shall be levied on the part of Government (as was heretofore done under the late Marhatta Government and as also been done under the British Government since the conquest of the province of Cuttack) on the pilgrims resorting to the temple of Juggernath".

"The collection of the tax shall be entrusted to an officer with the official designation of the Collector of the tax on pilgrims, subject to the authority of the Collector of Cuttack".*

An intermediate class known as *Nim Laal* was introduced. The Regulation IV of 1809 prescribed a certain number of days to different classes of pilgrims for access to the Temple. The Regulation IV of 1809 ended the direct administration of the Jagannath temple by the East India Company. It was a comprehensive measure, changing the system of the management of the Temple. It took into consideration the problems which arose after the imposition of the Pilgrim tax. It sought to restore the conditions which existed before the Marathas took over the management of the Temple. The Regulation vested the superintendence of the temple; and its internal economy and the control over the temple priests to the Raja of Khurda.

The British Government thus gave up the idea of appointing a committee of *pundits* to supervise the administration of the Temple. At the same time, restrictions were imposed on the authority of the Raja of Khurda. The Raja and his successors were to hold the position so long as they conducted themselves with integrity, diligence and propriety and were liable to removal by the Government on the ground of misconduct. The Raja was to be guided by the recorded rules of the Temple.

---

* The Regulations and Laws in Bengal, Vol. VI : Regulation IV of 1809. "The Regulation prescribes the rules for the management of the internal affairs of the Temple under the superintendence of the Rajah of Khoordah and specifies the Collector of Cuttack and Collector of tax as the European, authorized to interfere in the nomination of officers and to act as a check on the Rajah on the conduct of his duties subject to the orders of the Governor General in Council-the direct interposition of Government when necessary to restore good order appears to be throughout contemplated".

R. Ker, Commissioner to Government of India, Territorial Department: November 1818, Bengal Revenue Consultations, No. 21 National Library.

It was evident that the Raja of Khurda was mistrusted. It was apprehended that he might abuse the power which would be vested to him. The Government retained the power of appointing and dismissing the chief temple priests-the *Deul Parichhas*. They were given the right of checking any deviation from the customary usages and recorded rules of the temple on the part of the superintendent by making representation to the Collector of Cuttack. The Government also questioned the discretion of the Superintendent to exclude the persons whom he refrained from entering the temple.

Though the Raja of Khurda was given the management of the Temple affairs, the Government did not give up its close association with the Temple. The Government realised money from the pilgrims resorting to the temple of Jagannath, and fees from the "Pilgrim hunters" *Pundas* and the *Pratiharis*. It paid money for the establishment charges of the Temple and scrutinised the accounts.

Thus the Regulation of 1809 was a compromise between the views of the Board of Revenue supported by the Court of Directors, and of the Board of the Commissioners for the affairs of the temple. It introduced a Dyarchy in the administration of the Jagannath Temple. The superintendence of the temple was vested in the Raja of Khurda. But the Government reserved the right of supervision for the restoration of good order and prevention of irregularity in the Temple administration.

The collection of pilgrim tax in the beginning fell far short of expectation. In order to improve the situation one Mr. Busby was appointed as an assistant Collector on a salary of Rs. 300 per month with a commission of two per cent on the collection. The collection of pilgrim tax by the queen of Mayurbhanj State was abolished and the native military officers, sepoys, and servants of the European officers and the local pilgrims called Desees were exempted from payment of pilgrim tax.

The Jagannath road was in a deplorable condition and therefore the pilgrims belonging to upcountry and Bengal did not like to undertake the Journey. A good road along the old route was built with donations from Maharaja Sukhamoy Roy a *Zamindar* of Calcutta. Moreover, as recommended by the collector of pilgrim tax the walls of the temple which were in a bad shape were repaired. The expenses of these types of work necessitated imposition of pilgrim tax which was finally done in the interest of the Jagannath temple. Moreover, the British government took charge of the whole expenses of the temple which was of the order of Rs. 72438-6.

The Missionaries blamed the Government for collection of tax from the pilgrims visiting the Jagannath temple. They argued that the idolatrous worship in that temple would lapse without the Government support which implied in the collection of the pilgrim tax. On 6 June 1837 Rickets, commissioner wrote a letter to Wilkinson Collector of Puri regarding the proposal of abolition of the pilgrim tax and withdrawal of the Government interference in the affairs of the temple of Jagannath including the intention of the Government to rescind the Regulation IV of 1809 and XI of 1810. Rickets forwarded the letter of Wilkinson giving his suggestions in respect of future administration of the Jagannath temple. That the officers shall be relieved from interference in the internal affairs of the Jagannath temple by abolition of the Pilgrim tax. The *Sattais Hazari Mahal* be brought to the rent roll of the district. That an annual donation of Rs. 44776-6-6 shall be paid for the support of the temple. That the Superintendent Rajah Ramchandra Dev be vested by the Government with full powers in everything connected with the temple and its ceremonies and that small increase shall be allowed to the police establishment at Puri. On 20 April 1840 Act X of 1840 was passed which abolished the tax and fees upon the pilgrims resorting to Puri. It was provided in the Act that the Superintendence of the temple of Jagannath and its interior economy, the conduct and the management of its affairs and the control over the priests, officers and servants attached to the temple shall continue to be vested in the Raja of Khurda for the time being. The Collector, Puri wrote to Commissioner on 6 May 1840 acting upon the provision of Act X of 1840 as published in the Gazettee of 29 April I prohibited the collection of any tax from the pilgrims from 3 May. "At Puri on the 3rd May amidst the most tremendous storm in which the sacred wheel on the summit of the Pagoda tower was bent, the gate was thrown open and the pilgrims entered the barrier free".

Raja Birakishore Dev had to sign an agreement which would permanently alienate a portion of the State of Khurda. The Raja however did not like to sign the agreement but finally he had to sign the agreement under the force of the Government. Finally after official pressure put on the Raja he signed the deed before the Collector. The agreement gave legality to transactions by which by transferring land in lieu of money allowances, the Government discontinued payment of Jagannath temple from the treasury retaining only the control over the Jagannath temple Police establishment. By this there ended the rule of East India Company. The end of the East India Company's rule in India synchronised with the end of direct connection of the Christian Government with probably the most celebrated Hindu temple in India.

As pointed out earlier the East-India Company abolished the Pilgrim Tax and bypassing Act-X of the 1840 vested the then Raja of Puri with full authority in regard to the management of the temple and its properties. This Act prohibited the temple authorities to impose any restriction upon the pilgrims for admission into the temple and performing ceremonies free. At the same time the Government scrupulously maintained the pledges on the strength of which the temple continued to be under the protection of the Government. The Government made an annual payment to meet the expenses of the temple which was of the order of about Rs. 53,000 per year. In 1843, the Estate of Satais Hazari Mahal yielding an annual rent of Rs. 17,000 was made over to the Raja. Thereby the annual money payment made by the Government was reduced to Rs. 35,738. In 1845 it was ascertained that out of this sum Rs. 23,000 represented an assignment of revenue granted by the Raja of Berar and therefore the annual payment was further reduced to Rs. 23,321.

The Government found out the neglect by Birakishore Dev the then Raja superintendent of the temple of the management of the temple. In order to provide protection to the pilgrims the Government appointed a police establishment at an annual expense of Rs. 7,000 which was deducted from the Government grants to the temple. In 1858, the Government lands under Ekrajat Mahal were placed with the Raja in lieu of their cash payment to the temple. With the transfer of certain other lands yielding an equivalent grant of the Government, the Government ceased to have any connection with the management of the temple since the year 1863.

After the death of Birakishore Dev his widow Suryamoni Patamahadei took charge of the management of the temple because Divyasingh Dev the adopted son of Birakishore Dev was a minor at the time of the death of his adopted father. The management of the temple went from bad to worse and Divyasingh Dev was sentenced to transportation for life as he was accused of a murder case in 1878. When Divyasingh Dev was sentenced to transportation for life in 1877 his son Mukunda Dev was minor and therefore his grand-mother Suryamoni

Patmahadei acted as the guardian of her grand son. The mismanagement in the temple continued and the office of the superintendent of the temple was declared vacant. In such a situation a suit was filed in the court of law by the Government to get a decree for appointment of new trustees and for the settlement of a scheme for the management of the temple. The suit was compromised and the terms and conditions of the compromise are as follows:

(1) The management of Sri Jagannath temple which had been entrusted under Regulation IX/1809 and Act-X/1840 to the Raja of Khurda shall continue in hands of Mukunda Dev. But during his minority his grand-mother and guardian Rani Suryamoni Patmahadei was to act for him.

(2) During the period of her management Rani Suryamoni Patmahadei was to employ a competent manager and shall transfer to him all her powers over the Sebakas of the temple. But the manager could not remove any Sebaka without the consent of the Rani.

(3) If the Rani was to remove the manager she should appoint another manager within reasonable time and on default the civil court shall have power to appoint a competent manager to the said vacancy.

(4) This decree was to have no force after the Raja came of age.

This compromise was made in the year 1888, and it ceased to have any force by 1897 when Raja Mukunda Dev attained the age-after he came to age Mukunda Dev was recognized as Superintendent of the temple. Even during his time mismanagement continued in the affairs of the temple. Therefore, Raja Mukunda Dev was forced to take a Government Officer as Manager. Thus the management of the temple continued to be in the hands of Government servants of Gazetted rank. After the death of Raja Mukunda Dev in 1926 his adopted son Raja Ramachandra Dev took charge of the temple. After the death of Raja Ramachandra Dev came other Gajapati Rajas in the succession and acted as Raja superintendent of the temple, even after independence. This is just a brief outline of the history of the great institution which is unique in its nature and run by ancient traditions and visited by thousands of pilgrims almost everyday and even more on special festivals. Puri, the abode of Lord Jagannath, the God of Universe has been a pilgrim centre of national and even international repute.

The Pilgrim Tax in Different Periods

The Maratha Government was collecting pilgrim tax not only from the pilgrims coming to visit Lord Jagannath but also they were collecting the tax from those coming to visit sacred shrines. 12 *Caukis* (stations or centres) were established between Rajghat and Balasore for collection of tax from the pilgrims. This was the centre of Northern entrance through which the pilgrims coming from Bengal, Bihar, Uttarpradesh, Assam and other places were coming to Orissa to visit Lord Jagannath. The tax paid by those passing through northern gate used to pay Rs. 10/-and those coming from South paid Rs. 6/-per head. Those coming from south used to enter Puri town through Lokanath ghat and those coming from north enter via *Atharanalla ghat.* At both these *ghats* pilgrim tax was collected.

In addition to the payments of tax at the *ghats* the pilgrims used to pay tax at different places enroute to Puri. Some of these places are Balasore and Khunta located in Mayurbhanj border and as they approached Puri they had to pay tax at *Atharnalla* and *Lokanath* ghats as stated above. The pilgrims used to pay tax while passing through the territories of zamindars. Although the amount of tax to be paid by the pilgrims was fixed by the Government but it was not adhered to by the Tahsildars who were in charge of collection at different ghats. The amount of tax collected from the pilgrims was of the order of 2 to 5 lakhs of rupees annually.

In addition to the pilgrims tax the pilgrims had to pay a toll tax of 15 *annas* per head while entering the temple. The *Sanyasis*, and *Kangalas* were exempted from paying poll tax. At places the pious people built rest houses for the pilgrims to take rest. They also dug tanks and wells to supply water to the pilgrims. Many people and the chiefs of the States planted trees on the roadside for the pilgrims to take rest under such trees. The places at Balasore and Bhadrak were dangerous because at such places the robbers used to plunder the travellers and made them destitutes (*Kangalas*). The robbers used some intoxicating preparations and applied into the nostrils of tired pilgrims to make them senseless and sleep sound sleep. When they woke up in the morning they woke up stark naked because even the clothes they put on were stripped off from their body by the robbers.

The Jagannath Temple was a great source of income for the Maratha Government. When the British took over the administration of the temple the Maratha Government put up a strong fight against the British interference. But finally the Maratha Government had to quit. However in the interim period certain conditions were provided in the treaty between the British rule and the outgoing Maratha regime.

The conditions are as follows :

1. The Jagannath Pagoda and all the duties collected from the pilgrims shall remain to the Marathas.

2. A Maratha governor will be posted in the temple and he will have supreme authority over the functionaries and the pilgrims visiting the temple.

3. The villages and the landed properties which were allocated during Maharaja Janugi's governance for the support of the Brahmins of Brahmin Settlements shall remain under the control of the Marathas.

4. The religious ceremonies which were performed annually by the pilgrims in the Jagannath temple shall be continued and two officials posted in the temple to collect duties or fees which the pilgrims used to pay on these ritual occasions and make payments to the Marathas.

5. All villages and lands formerly donated to the Brahmins should remain in their possession as before.

6. Moral Pandit and Sewaji Pandit who were appointed before as *Parichha* in the Jagannath temple should continue in their posts as usual even after the Maratha were withdrawn when the British took over administration of Orissa in 1803 AD.

From year after year the Anglo-Maratha conflict arose on different fronts and it got intensified as the years passed by and finally it ended in the war which was declared against the Maratha Government on 3rd August 1802 AD. and the British took over the administration of Orissa in 1803 AD including the management and control of the Jagannath temple.

Briefly speaking, during the administration of the Marathas in Orissa, they treated the pilgrims to Jagannath with a degree of attention and consideration. It was of course their interest to do so. To take particular care about the collection of the pilgrim tax-to entice as many pilgrims as possible and to afford them the protection of the State, while they enjoyed their devotion in the holy land. It was a portion of their policy. The pilgrim hunters of the latter half of the 18th century must have found little difficulty in causing multitude to undertake pilgrimage.

In conclusion, Laurie observed "yet these people in the gradual sunset of their glory, even with their rapacity and violence must have commanded a considerable portion of their veneration. They adhered strictly to the rule of Brahma. This, in the eyes of the people of Orissa, must have covered a multitude of sins".

Jagannath Temple Administration After Independence

The temple of Lord Jagannath at Puri is an Institution well-known throughout India and elsewhere. Its national importance is so great that it needs no mention to the public of India. For better administration of the Temple and its affairs and to prevent mismanagement thereof which unfortunately has appeared since the last few years, the Government of Orissa as a preliminary step towards undertaking a comprehensive legislation about the temple, have passed Act XIV of 1952 providing for appointment of a special officer to consolidate and prepare record-of rights and duties of the various classes of *Sebakas* and other persons connected with the *Seba Puja* of the Temple. The necessity for this legislation can very well be gathered from the statement of objects and reasons given by the Hon'ble Shri D. Sahu, the Minister, Law and Home, while introducing the Bill in the Assembly :

Statement of Objects and Reasons

"The Puri Temple of Lord Jagannath which occupies an unique position not only in the State of Orissa but also in relation to the whole of the union is in a sad plight.

Abject mismanagement, a standing disgrace to the citizens and their administration, prevails in spite of all efforts to remedy it. There is no escape but that in the interest of the public, State Government must step in and take effective measures in order to save it from ruination.

In the absence of any guidance from the Raja and sufficient contribution from him for the regular expenses of the Temple, the scheduled and disciplined performance of the *Nitis* has suffered beyond imagination and the Raja has practically lost all control over the different *Sebakas* and other temple servants.

Economic rivalry and moral degeneration of the servants and Sebaks has divested them of all sense of duty and cooperation. Specific endowments are regularly misapplied and misappropriated. Strikes amongst various classes are of common occurrence. The non-availability at the appointed hours of the Mahaprasad coveted and adored by millions of pilgrims is always there in these days. The lapses into unorthodoxy has resulted in extremely unhygienic conditions inside the temple and commission of heinous crimes even within the Temple precincts is not rare even the image of the deity has been at times defiled and its precious jewellery removed. Peace and solemnity inside the temple has given way to sheer goondaism and it is mainly the servants of the temple that make up the unruly elements responsible for such lawless state of affairs.

For the purpose of exercising effective supervision over the administration of the Temple and its endowments, a

Bill was prepared and introduced in the State Legislature in June 1948. Provisions for constitution of a Committee with the Raja of Puri as Chairman ex officio, was made for an effective administration of all the religious and specific endowments-jewels and the properties vested in the deity subject to the control of the State Government. Provisions for constitution of a council of religious rituals was also made to settle disputes regarding rituals in the temple. This committee was required under the said bill to report upon disputes relating to the rights of Sebaks, etc., and to control the daily time-table relating to the performance of ceremonies in the temple. This bill further provided for giving loans by the State Government to the funds of the temple for proper administration of the same. This bill was not however enacted and reasons are not known. The fact remains that the Bill fell through perhaps due to constitutional difficulties. All efforts from 1937 to 1948 to enact legislations have still failed due to initial difficulties as to the nature of rights and duties of the principal persons interested in the Seba Puja of the deity and other idols.

In the result, the failure of these above attempts has mainly been due to the fact that no proper efforts have yet been made to have an authenticated record of different individuals and classes of persons on whom the various rights and duties in the complex scheme of Seba Puja has from time immemorial devolved. Even there has never been a proper assessment of the position of the Raja visa-vis the deity. The state legislature do not propose to interfere so as to alter the existing services. But preserving all that in tact, the proper carrying out of the scheme by emphasising the details of the administration of the properties and the income of the deity and enforcing accordingly each and every item of activity enjoined on the respective persons is undoubtedly feasible. The different *Sebakas* may have the full liberty of managing the religious affairs of the institution but it is as pointed out above in the interest of the public that their propensity to mismanage such affairs of the institution should in no manner be tolerated and so far as law allows, the state must intervene.

This obviously can only be effected by a specific legislation directed to meet the peculiar needs of the situation and any half-hearted measures will be of no avail. Such legislation must aim at making all manner of default on the part of the temple servant an offence punishable with fine and every strike illegal, the fines being appropriated towards the funds of the temple. This is the least that can be provided for as a preventive measure.

But before that final stage of legislation can be launched upon and made effective and even be justifiable, it would be absolutely necessary, firstly, to have it determined the nature of all services that are to be rendered; secondly, the individuals on whom the liability of such performance rests; and thirdly, the rights and privileges attached to such services. It is then only that it would be possible to apply with any precision the preventive measures by penalising the defaults.

A legislative process was proposed to provide for the preparation of a record-of-rights and duties by an officer appointed by Government for the purpose. The steps taken in this regard are discussed in the following chapters.

Puri as a Pilgrim Centre

Before describing about the pilgrimage to Puri in the past and in contemporary period it is necessary to go into the question of since when did Puri became a famous pilgrim centre and the idol became so celebrated as to attract hundreds of Pilgrims from different parts of the country. The antiquity of Puri and the cult of Jagannath are still shrouded in history. In specific terms to fix the time of the importance of Jagannath in Puri town is quite impossible. Puri was known in the past as *Purusottama Khetra*, because the presiding deity of this *khetra* was formerly known as *Purusottama* and by virtue of the name and fame of this deity the Purusottama Khetra has been enjoying a position as one of the foremost religious centres of India. Besides this name Purusotama Khetra the city is also known as *Niladri*, *Sri Khetra*, *Sankha Khetra*, *Jamnika Khetra* and *Martya Baikuntha*. So great is the majesty of the presiding deity which goes by the name Jagannath that all people are equal before him, and all social distinction of caste and creed and nationality disappear in the presence of his greatness and sanctity. The cult of Jagannath is considered to be the embodiment of various sects and therefore Puri is considered to be *Sarva Dharma Samanwaya Dhama* which is taken as one of the seven *Mokshapuris* or salvation city of the Hindu faith.

As mentioned above the history of Purusottama Khetra or the cult of Purusottama Jagannath is of great antiquity. The *Kapila Sanhita* refers to the Purusottama Khetra as the one that takes away sin. The *Matsya Purana* which is one of the oldest *puranas* has a reference to Purusottam but there is no mention of Jagannath. But the Puranas which came later on make references to Jagannath as a presiding deity of the Purusottama Khetra.

Jagannath makes his first appearance in history in 318 A.D., when the priests fled away with his image to escape the wrath of *Raktabahu* and his army. After about 150 years later the holy log of the image of Jagannath was recovered by a noble prince. Murari Mishra has given reference to Lord Purusottama who was being worshipped on the seashore. That there was an earlier temple of Jagannath at *Purusottama Khetra* prior to the present one built by Chodaganga Deb in 12th Century A.D. One point which requires mention regarding the antiquity of Purusottama Jagannath is that Anncharlott Eschmann, Hermann Kulke and Gaya Charan Tripathi have mentioned in the book the Cult of Jagannath and the Regional Tradition of Orissa that "the entire early period of 600 years from the 4th century to the beginning of the 10th century A.D. there is not even the slightest hint in any inscriptional or archaeological sources of the existence of a Purusottama Khetra in Orissa or of a Jagannath temple on the seashore. But in the '*tirthayatra*' section of *Vanaparva* of Mahabharata there is a mention of *Svayambhu Lokesvara* and the *Vedi*, a famous spot in Puri itself, thus testifying to the antiquity of Puri as a place on the pilgrim's route" L.S.S. O' Malley in Bihar and Orissa district Gazetters, Puri has mentioned, "The Jagannath Pilgrimage appears to be at least eight centuries old, for in an inscription dating back in 1137 A.D. We find mention of a pilgrim who went to the sacred Purusottama Khetra and gave away his wealth in charity on the noisy shore of the sea." Throughout these centuries the magnificence of the temple, with its elaborate rituals, the liberal royal patronage it enjoyed, the development of Vaishnavism, the catholicity of worship it inculcated, have combined in attracting attention to Jagannath and year after year a steady stream of pilgrims has flowed to the temple by the sea inspite of the great difficulties of the journey.

Thus it shows that pilgrimage to Puri was of great antiquity. No inscriptions refer to the present temple, the construction of which probably started after 1135 A.D. The Madala Panji's tradition is that an older dilapidated temple was pulled down in order to build the present temple. Thus there existed a famous Purusottam temple in Puri during the Somavansi rule Mahasivagupta Yayati Kesari II (cir AD 1023-1040) 11th century and it was widely known since the middle of the 11th century. As stated above under the liberal royal patronage of the dynasties which followed the temple became famous and widely known as a great pilgrim centre which was visited by thousands of pilgrims from different parts of the country. For example, Ananga Bhima Dev III (1198-1223) built the present Jagannath temple and appointed different categories of ritual functionaries called *chhatisanijog* performing different ritual services in the *sebapuja* of the Lord Jagannath.

After the rulers of Ganga dynasty came Kesari dynasty, Surya dynasty, and Bhoi dynasty which succeeded Somavansi rulers in succession donated vast landed properties, established Sasan villages and donated precious stones, Jewellery and ornaments, etc. which enhanced the fame of the deities and the temple and attracted thousands of pilgrims from different parts of the country during festivals and on many ritual occasions throughout the year.

This famous temple of Lord Jagannath also known as Sri Mandir stands on the holy ground of *Sri Khetra* or *Purusottam Khetra* and also described as *Sankha Khetra.* Located between Lat. 19°18' and 17" N and Long. 85° 51' and 39" E, this majestic edifice is 214.66 feet in height from the ground level standing on a raised platform of stone (area 420000 sqft.) and surrounded by an outwall known as *Meghanada Pacheri* of 665 ft in length and six metres in height as well as by an inner wall *Kurma Bedha* of 420 feet in length. The sanctum-sanctorum contains the *Ratna Bedi* (throne of chlorite) and over this five-feet high platform are seated the three deities Balaram, Subhadra and Jagannath. Within the inner compound there are several shrines, small temples, sacred trees and other sacred places which the pilgrims visit during their pilgrimage to Puri. The Kendupatna copper plates give credit to Codaganga (1078-1147 A.D.) as the builder of the present temple of Lord Jagannath.

One word may be mentioned regarding how and when the*Purusottama Khetra* came to be known and called as Puri. The Europeans referred to it as "*Jekanat*" or "*Jaggarnat*". After the British conquest the town was sometimes called "*Jaggarnath-Poore*". Mr. W. Hamilton in his description of Hindustan (1820) mentioned the place as "*Jaggarnati*", "*Jaggarnathpoor*" and "Poore". Sterling in his account of Orissa (1824) used both "Jagarnnath-Poore" and simply "Pooree". Later the term Pooree was abbreviated and changed to simply Puri which is being used since the last half of the 19th century.

L.S.S.O' Malley in Bihar and Orissa District Gazetteers Puri (1929) mentioned The Jagannath Pilgrimage appears to be at least eight centuries old (p. 124). It is certain that after the construction of the present temple of Jagannath during the period of Anantavarman Codaganga Deva sometime between 1135 A.D. and Mid-12th century A.D., the pilgrimage to Puri must have increased considerably. That there was an earlier temple of Jagannath at Purusottam Khetra prior to the present one built by Codaganga Deva in 12th century AD is proved by the mention of Davayatana of God Purusottama in Krishna Mishra's Prabodha Chandrodaya Natakam (c. 1078 AD). Thus it is probable that pilgrimage to Puri may have taken place much earlier to 12th century AD.

In any case the pilgrimage to Puri is something of great antiquity and it is impossible to deal with this subject since that time. Considering the limitations of time and financial provisions the study is confined to a period beginning from the Mughal rule through Maratha administration to the British Raj extended to the present time. The description of pilgrimage during the first two periods, that is, the Mughal and Maratha periods is sketchy whereas that of the later periods, that is, the British rule and post British contemporary period has been somewhat elaborately dealt with.

The Pilgrims

As already mentioned that Pilgrimage to reputed holy places have ever been so popular in India, but no pilgrimage was ever so extensively practiced and so generally famed as that of pilgrimage to Jagannath. The legend relating to discovery of Jagannath by *Bidyapati* in a forest where *Biswabasu* was worshipping him and the construction of temple in the seashore at Puri for instalation of the deity in the temple. Consecration of the temple and the deity by Brahma himself who came down to Puri on invitation from the then Raja *Indradyumna* and royal patronage that the Puri temple received from the Hindu kings from one dynasty to another are some of the circumstances which made the idol most sacred and celebrated and widely known in the country. Thousands and thousands of pilgrims including famous saints like Sankaracharya, Chaitanya, Ramanuja, Kabir, Nanaka and many others of different sects came on pilgrimage to Puri during festivals and other ritual occasions which are observed at Puri. For the last 10 centuries covering the period of Ganga dynasty up to the present day the temple has stood in the shore of Bay of Bengal, with the Lord of Universe, Lord Jagannath. Here is the national temple whither thousands and thousands of pilgrims coming from every part of the country even from abroad flock together to worship Lord Jagannath. Groome, one of the Collector of Puri appointed by the British Government in the year 1803 has given an elaborate account of the pilgrims resorting to the temple of Jagannath.

The pilgrims used to come from different directions. Those coming from the north passed through a place called *Khunta* on the border of Mayurbhanj state and continued upto Atharanalla at the entrance of Poorshuttam or Puri. The pilgrims coming from the south were entering the holy city through Lokanath. These entry points such as the Atharanalla Ghat and Lokanath Ghat were set up enabling the officers stationed at those places to collect the tax from the pilgrims. The number of pilgrims coming on pilgrimage to Puri runs to thousands. Of all the festivals the Car festival attract.thousands of pilgrims from all corners of the country.

Types of Pilgrims

There are many types of pilgrims depending upon their economic condition, sect affiliation, nativity. An account of different types of pilgrims is given below:

1. *Panchakosi Jatri*

These pilgrims belong to Puri town and the neighbouring areas covering the villages within 5 *Kosas* (10 kms.). Specifically the area covers upto Pipli in the north Konark in the east. Brahmagiri in the west. Of course the area which comes under *Panchakosi* may be more than 5 *Kosas*. The pilgrims of *Panchakosi* have no specified Pandas nor they used to pay any pilgrim tax in the past.

2. *Pancha tirtha Jatri*

The pilgrims belonging to this category were untouchables. They came only to go to *panchtirthas* located in Puri town. The places under Panchatirthas are (1) *Markanda*, (2) *Swetaganga*, (3) *Mahodadhi*, (4) *Chakratirtha*, (5) *Indradyumna*. They used to pay only Rs. 4/-towards the pilgrim tax and had *Darshan* of the *panchtirthas* with the help of *Choukidars*.

3. *Desi Jatri*

The pilgrims coming from the area which covers the Baitarani river in Jajpur district were called *Desi Jatri*. They are also exempted from the pilgrim tax.

4. *Lal Jatri*

The Jatris belonging to this category were the richest of all categories of the pilgrims. When they come via Atharanalla they used to pay tax at the rate of Rs. 10/-per head and Rs. 6/-per head if they came via Lokanath ghat.

They were allowed to stay at Puri for a period of 30 days. The permit ticket which was issued to them were of red colour. They were permitted to go to the temple holding *Chamar* (whisk) in day time and *Masal* (torch) at night.

5. *Nim lal Jatri*

The pilgrims used to pay tax at the rate of Rs. 5/-per head if they came from North via Atharanalla and Rs. 3-if they came from south Via Lokanath ghat.

6. *Bhurunga Jatri*

The pilgrims used to pay tax at the rate of Rs. 2/-per head if they came via Atharanalla. They were permitted to stay in Puri town for only 4 days.

7. *Khairati Jatri*

The pilgrims who are local people, Government servants, poor people, destitutes, diseased, police, sipahi, and messengers, belong to this category and they were exempted from payment of any tax.

8. *Gangajali Jatri*

The pilgrims of this category used to carry water from the rive Ganges and pour them on the deity Lokanath and then have *darshan* of the Lord Jagannath and there after go back home. They were exempted from payment of any tax.

9. *Bairagi Jatri*

The *Sanyasi*, diseased, destitutes, and those having no shelter anywhere like wandering *sanyasis*, a mad persons who came under this category did not have to make any payment of taxes.

10. *Dandabhanga Jatri*

The *Jatri* of this category covers the journey not by walking but by means prostrating his body on the road and then getting up and again prostrating. This way he covers the distance from the point he left for pilgrimage until he reached his destination, that is, Puri.

11. *Pousa Gaya Jatri and Gangasar Jatri*

After offering manes to the ancestors at Gaya the pilgrims visit Puri on pilgrimage to have *darshan* of the Lord Jagannath.

12. *Mala Jatri*

The pilgrims belonging to different parts of the country and even some of them coming from abroad came on pilgrimage to Puri. Generally the pilgrims took help of *Jatri Pandas* and *Jatri Gumsthas* for *Darshan* of the deity and for going round *Sri Kshetra* to touch upon the sacred places and sacred objects. For the services rendered by the *Pandas* and their assistance, they made some payments to them according to their means. But these categories of pilgrims did not take any help from the Pandas nor they paid anything to them. Therefore the Pandas have given them as name as Malajatri or dead pilgrims.

Like the above mentioned divisions of the pilgrims there were also divisions according to their nativity. There divisions are:

1. *Jaleswar Jatri* : Those *Jatris* coming from the northern localities of the Mahanadi river were designated as such.

2. *Southern Mahajatri* : The pilgrims coming from Singhbhum, Gujarat, Agartala, Gaurakumuti, Kendujharia, Budia, Bundeli were called southern *mahajatri*.

3. *Western Jatri* : The *Jatris* coming under this category belonged to Marahatta, Nagpur, Garhmandala, Chhatisgarh, Sambalpur, Ranpur, Kamatelenga, Shri Baishnaba, Kalahandi, Bastar, Raipur, Jaypur, Raygada, Gunpur, Paratikali, Tarala, Badakhemundi, Jarada, Manjusa, Mahuri, Sorada, Seragarh, Ghumsar.

For collection of taxes and for regulation of tax collection centres were established at Narsinghpur, Jobra, Gundichaghar, Mangalaghat, Lokanath ghat, Atharanala, and Puri sadar office. Besides these centres Khunta of Mayurbhanj was also a place where a collection centre was established permit cards were issued to the *Jatris* for entry into Puri town. Also exit cards were issued while leaving Puri town. This permit card issued for their return journey was called *Khalasi* letter.

Pilgrimage to Puri, Pandas and their Pilgrim Business

Many years back there was no road communication to Puri. But thousands of pilgrims from different parts of the country used to come on pilgrimage to see the car festivals and the Jagannath temple at Puri. Those coming from North India used to take routes via-Bihar and Chhotanagpur and those coming from eastern India come via Lakshmanabati and Cuttack. Those coming from southern India used to come via Ganjam through coastal area and Chilika lake. Many of them had to come by boat through Hoogly, Baleswar, Masalipatna, Similipatna, Barrua, Chilka lake.

In order to develop road communication the British authorities started the construction of the Jagannath road in 1822 to 1826. The Raja of Calcutta Sukhamaya Deb donated about one and a half lakh of rupees. In spite of lack of good communication about 53 thousands of pilgrims visited Puri on Pilgrimage in the year 1839. This number increased to 1.12.000 in 1842, and it further increased to 2,10,000 in the year 1861 during the car festival. Inspite of such difficulties of road communication the Pandas and their Gumasthas used to go out 5 to 6 months before the festival took place to their respective areas and villages to meet their pilgrims, spread the Jagannath cult and invite them to come to Puri during the coming car festival. Thousands and thousands of pilgrims used to come to Puri on foot covering hundreds of miles from their respective villages through forests and rough and rugged terrain. As a result of such arduous journey many pilgrims had to sustain injuries in their body and also meet death on the way. Mr. John beams, the then Collector of Balaswar had a descriptive eye witness account of the pilgrims journey on Calcutta-Madras Trunk Road to Puri to witness the Car festival in the year 1860. This descriptive account is available in a book called Memories of Bengal civilian.

A List of the Important Pandas and their Pilgrim Ilakas (areas)

	Name of Jatri Panda	*Native Place*	*Area under their Jurisdiction*
1/1	Ramachandra Gochhikara	Harachandi Sahi	Gujarat
2/2	Artatrana Mahasuara	Harachandi Sahi	Maharastra
3/3	Balabhadra Gochhikara	Harachandi Sahi	Hariyana
7/4	Ramachandra Pratihari Pancha Bhai Gobardhana	Harachandi Sahi	Jhansi Lalita Bina, Kari
8/5	Lokanath Pratihari (Kabara Ghoda)	Harachandi Sahi	Banda, Himrpur, Sindubad
13/6	Lokanath Gangadhara Mahapatra	Harachandi Sahi	Rayagada, Saranga, Bilaspur, Raypur
14/7	Anata Mahapatra	Harachandi Sahi	Nepal, Assam
15/8	Banamali Mahapatra	Harachandi Sahi	Manipur 45%
17/9	Shrinath Khuntia	Harachandi Sahi	Allahabad, Lucknow
21/10	Dwarikanath Khuntia	Harachandi Sahi	Allahabad

(Contd.)

(Table Contd.)

	Name of Jatri Panda	Native Place	Area under their Jurisdiction
26/11	Ramanath Khuntia	Harachandi Sahi	Bankuda Grama
31/12	Balakrushna Mahapatra	Harachandi Sahi	Sambalpur
34/13	Ramanarayana Khuntia	Harachandi Sahi	2 or 3 district of Rajasthan
5/14	Kalijuga Damodara Pratihari		Punjab, Jammu
22/15	Jayaram Sinhari		
6/16	Bade Harihara (Guru Estate) Rabi Narayana Guru, Prasana Guru	Goudabada Sahi	Bihar
33/17	Mahadeba Pujapanda	Gudia Sahi	Berhampur
10/18	Telenga Padhiari	Balisahi	South India
11/19	Narasingh Nath Daitapati	Dolamandap Sahi	Medinipur
20/20	Gopal Khuntia	Dolamandap Sahi	West Bengal
23/21	Kashinath Sinhari	Dolamandap Sahi	Kanpur town
24/22	Chintamani Sinhari	Dolamandap Sahi	Chari sampradaya
25/23	Niranjana Sinhari	Dolamandap Sahi	West Bengal, Banki (Orissa)
28/24	Jagannath Puspalaka	Dolamandapa Sahi	Angul (Orissa)
12/25	Raghunath Sinhari	Talucha Sahi	Chhatisgarh
27/26	Raghunath kar	Talucha Sahi	Madhya Pradesh
32/27	Bhubana Mohana Kar	Hajuri Lane	Athagada
16/28	Chandan Hajuri	Harachandi Sahi	Pradap Gada
18/29	Arjuna Sadangi	Baseli Sahi	Rajasthan
19/30	Mahabir Khuntia	Markendeswar Sahi	West Bengal
29/31	Bhagabana Mahapatra	Balisahi, Bahari lane	Dhenkanal
4/32	Chhota Gobardhana Jagannath Mahapatra	Gochikara Sahi	Delhi
8/33	Kashinath/Biswanath Padhiari (Choudha bhai babda)	Bhind, Morena	Gwalior
30/34	Chintamani Kar	Talucha Sahi	Talcher

Life of the Pilgrims at Puri

Being a famous Vaisnavite Tirtha of the 12th century Puri, originally known as Purushottam Kshetra or Jagannath *Dham*, attracts thousands of pilgrims from all Indo-Aryan regions of the country. Their number runs to millions during the car festival. The earliest record of pilgrimage to Puri dates back to 1137 A.D. A pilgrim visited this sacred centre in that year and gave away all his wealth to the temple.

The Panda and Pratihari sebakas have divided different areas of the country among themselves and visit those areas with *Nirmalya* (rice grains half cooked in the temple kitchen), and *Mahaprasad* call upon their clients and give them prasad and bring them to Puri on a short visit in pilgrimage during festivities such as car festival, *Chandan* and *Dol jatra*. The prosperous and influential Pandas have employed agents or *Gumasthas* to perform journey on their behalf and fetch the pilgrims to Puri.

The assistants of the Pandas are of two classes : *Deswari* or *Batua* who go out to different parts of the country and fetch their pilgrims and *Ghatua* who are pilgrim touts remaining at Puri and contacting pilgrims at the railway station and at other points of entry into Puri town.

The British Government levied a tax on the pilgrims reporting to the temple of Sri Jagannath under the Regulation IV, 1806 A.D. Later the Regulation V, 1806 A.D. was passed for checking persons who evaded payment of the tax.

In Regulation IV, 1809 A.D., the entry points were specified and accordingly the pilgrims were admitted into Puri through these points. Two avenues for the admission of the pilgrims were specified, that is Atharanalla Ghat on the north and Lokanath Ghat on the south-west of Puri town. According to the categories to which the pilgrims belong the amount of the tax to be paid by each class of pilgrims, duration of their stay and access to the temple etc., were specified in the Regulation.

In the year 1840 the East India Company felt that the money received in the form of Pilgrim Tax was to a certain extent the price of a State sanction to idolatry and accordingly the company abolished the Pilgrim Tax and by passing the Act X, 1840 the temple authorities were forbidden to impose any restrictions upon the pilgrims for admission into Puri town and into the temple to pay homage to the deities.

From a very early time the pilgrims from different directions of the compass representing different parts of the country have been visiting in thousands on pilgrimage to Puri. According to them Puri is nothing but a heaven upon earth. In specific terms what they believe about Puri has already been mentioned elsewhere. Thousands of Pilgrims coming from far off and near by places witness the car festival at Puri. The scene of multitudinous of pilgrims during car festival has been vividly described by David B. Smith, M.D. Sanitary Commissioner for Bengal during his visit to Puri in 1868. The narrative of his visit is as follows :

"I had been anxious to get to this celebrated place before dark; but this I found to be impossible. My first view of the city was by starlight. As I passed up its principal street-the "*Burra Dund*" which is nearly a mile long and very broad, I observed, chiefly at the far end of it, many thousands of pilgrims lying on the ground, sleeping quietly; there was no noise; here and there a small wick lamp was burning, which had been lit by one of a party of individuals lying huddled together, a little apart from the rest of the slumbering crowd. The scene was peculiarly impressive.

Those numberless men and women, enjoying much-needed repose, had come together from every point of the compass, many of them from very distant places, all actuated by the one burning desire to reach Juggernauth. Here at last they had accomplished their desire, and wearied with the accumulated fatigue of many marches, they lay in perfect stillness on the bare ground, Not a sound was to be heard; the stars yielded faint light, and before me I saw, as if in dreamland, an army of religious enthusiasts, who, in the fervour of a fanatical creed, had completed a pilgrimage which, to the Hindoo mind, is the surest viaticum to a happier state of being."

While narrating the hardship and strain the pilgrims had undergone in their journey Smith had further said.

"During the Rath Jatra festival, those who come together are for the most part Bengalees, of whom a very large proportion are women. While I was passing along the crowd I observed a party of up-country men, I spoke to them, and found that they were Punjabees who had just come down all the way from Hazara, some 2,000 miles. They told me that they had been travelling four and five months, that they were going to stay a day or two at Juggernauth, and then at once return to their homes. Shakespear's words were recalled to my mind :

> *"A true-hearted pilgrim does not fear to measure kingdoms with his feeble-steps".*

More vivid and pathetic was the description of Sir W.W. Hunter regarding the journey of the pilgrims to Puri. A paragraph from his description is quotated below:

"The great spiritual army marched in hundreds sometimes thousands of miles along burning roads, across unbridged rivers, and through pestilent regions of jungle and swamps. Those who kept to the road had spent their strength long before the holy city was reached. The sturdy women of Hindustan braved it out and sang songs till they dropped; but the weaker females of Bengal limped piteously along with bleeding feet in silence, broken only by deep sighs and an occasional sob. Many a sickly girl died upon the road; and by the time they reached Puri, the whole party had their feet bound up in rags, plastered with dirt and blood (Puri District Gazetteer, 1929, by L.S.S. O'Malley p. 128)".

The pilgrims pour into Puri from all directions most of them waling the distance from home to Puri. As road communications developed people came by bullock carts, along the Jagannath Trunk Road and also by rail. In this connection a paragraph from the Puri District Gazetteer, 1929, by L.S.S.O'Malley, p. 125 is reproduced below:

"At that time the Bengal pilgrims had to tramp all the way from Uluberia to Puri on the Jagannath Trunk Road. Only the wealthier classes travelling in bullock carts or palanquins, while pilgrims from the south used to come by road along the strip of land between the Chilika lake and the Bay, or in a few cases by boats across the Chilika lake. During the last thirty years of the nineteenth century the difficulties of the journey were much decreased, as it was possible to go from Calcutta by sea-going steamers to Chandabali in the Balasore district, and thereafter by the river up to Cuttack, and lastly by road to Puri. Now-a-days most pilgrims travel by rail direct to the sacred town. Even after the roads were developed some pilgrims are even now seen measuring their length prostrate along the road, all the way from their home for scores of miles."

The Pilgrim-Pandas and their agents take care of the pilgrims at Puri. The pilgrims of different areas are attached to different Pandas. As soon as the pilgrims arrive at Puri their respective Pandas lodge them in dharmasalas and lodging houses, arrange for supply of mahaprasad daily and depute men to show them round particularly the sacred places. Those pilgrims who land up at Puri without escort by any pilgrim-guides or agents of Pandas fall into difficulties. They are questioned by the Pandas, and the registers maintained by the Pandas are looked into to trace out the ancestors or any relations of these pilgrims. These registers are called Panda's book in which the names of pilgrims and details about their native places and date of visit to Puri are recorded. When no record of a pilgrim is traced out there is often a brawl, a fight between two Pandas each claiming the pilgrim as his client and in the long run the mightier wins the case. In this connection David B. Smith has also given a pathetic description in his report on Pilgrimage to Puri.

The pilgrimage to Puri as observed by Smith not only entailed incalculable misery, suffering and loss of life, in the journey but it was also a history of disease and death which the Pilgrims met at Puri. Under what unhygienic and insanitary conditions the pilgrims were crammed into the lodging houses in the earlier days will be clearly understood from the following paragraphs which are reproduced from the Smith's report pp. 3-5.

The pilgrims at Pooree are so densely crowded in every apartment, that it is simply impossible to admit more inmates; not only the corners and the centre of a lodging house are occupied, but the entire space was full of pilgrims. One Dr. Mouat has described one of these terrible places :-

"In the lodging-houses they are crowded to such an extent, that I was shown one apartment, in the best pilgrim hotel of the place, in which eighty persons were said to have passed the night. It was thirteen feet long, ten feet five inches broad, with side walls six feet and a half in height, and a low pent roof over it. It had but one entrance, and no ventilation worthy of note. It was dark, dirty and dismal when quite empty, and must have been a rest house during the festivals. In this house, in a similar room, occurred the first case of cholera of the last outbreak. If this be the normal state of the best lodging-house in the broad main street of Pooree, it is not difficult to imagine the condition of the worst, in the narrow, confined, undrained, back-slums of the town-for there are lower depths even in this abode of filth and corruption".

"Most of the Pandas have houses of their own for the reception of pilgrims. When these are fully occupied, other places are rented, at high charges, in which pilgrims are crowded almost to suffocation. In apartments containing 50 or 100 people, there is very little light, less pure air, and no ventilation".

The following is an extract from the diary of the Deputy Inspector General of Police, for the week ending 16th November, 1867 :-

"The District Superintendent writes :-I went into a house in the town this afternoon; above 45 pilgrims were putting up, men and women; the place had only two doors, no windows (one of the doors was locked). This place measured 12 by 20 feet, certainly not more; and in this place no less than 45 persons were crammed. The stench was overpowering and the heat like an oven; no wonder the people are attacked with cholera; and unless some law is passed to prevent these Pandas overcrowding their houses with pilgrims, not only cholera but other diseases are sure to be generated".

Mr. Raban, the Magistrate and Collector of Pooree, thus alludes to this subject in his admirable Report to the Commissioner of Cuttack (No. 93 T dated 19th February, 1968) :-"The poorer up-country pilgrims submit to crowed rooms : but the Oriya pilgrims crowd into a room till it would be difficult to introduce another person. I visited one room filled with Oriyas from Kimedy, in the Madras Presidency; the room was so crowded that it was difficult to move, yet several of the people were singing, and one was actually cooking for the rest at a large fire, which filled the room with smoke. This was an extreme case, but I satisfied myself, by visiting a number of houses, that the people are crowded in a manner prejudicial to health, and calling for special legislation. Many of the houses afford very fair accommodation for limited numbers, but are quite unfit for the reception of the number that crowd into them. A third class railway carriage, filled with native passengers, gives a very fair idea of the extent of the crowding; and it must be recollected that these people sleep in these crowded rooms, which are no better provided with ventilation that the ordinary kind of houses in this country".

"Giving heed to these observations of eye-witnesses, and remembering that a single individual breathes 1616 cubic feet of air in an hour, and that in that time he should be supplied with a fresh supply equal to nearly 2,000 cubic feet, we are in a position to estimate the dreadfully abnormal conditions of the interiors of Pooree lodging-houses".

Shocked by the alarming report of Dr. Smith and others a bill was brought before the Lieutenant Governor's council on the 15th December 1866 for better regulation of lodging houses at Puri. The most important points mentioned in the bill were the following suggestions for the improvement in sanitary conditions, the suggestions are 1) The appointment of a Health Officer and the management of the lodging houses only by license holders, 2) imposition of fines on lodging houses only by license holders, imposition of fines on lodging house keepers not taking out a license and keeping the lodging house in insanitary conditions and periodic inspection of lodging house in sanitary conditions and 3) periodic inspection of lodging houses by health officer.

Subsequently a committee called Pilgrim Committee was formed with the Collector/Magistrate and leading persons of the town, representatives of sebaka communities and Mahantas of selected monasteries to control and regulate pilgrim traffic. The arrangements made by the committee are as follows :

1. The district Magistrate shall issue licenses to such number of persons as he thinks fit to act or be employed as a Panda remaining in charge of lodging houses. The District Magistrate may delegate this power to any of his subordinate officers.

2. Any Sebak or person connected with the *seba puja* or worship of Jagannath is entitled to act or be employed as a Panda provided he be of good character.

3. Any respectable person of good character may be employed by any *Panda* as his *Gumasta* or agent and may take out a license to act as such through his employer.

4. The licence granted to a Panda shall ordinarily be for life and shall be chargeable with a fee of Rs. 15.

5. The *Gumastas* can be divided into two classes:-

   (a) *Deswari* or *Batua* that is, those that go out to differnt parts of India to fetch pilgrims.

(b) *Ghatua*, that is, those who meet and tout for pilgrims at Puri and neighbouring railway stations.

As a rule these two classes are quite distinct from each other, and separate licenses might be granted to them according to the nature of the duties which they have to perform. The license granted to a *Gumasta* of either kind shall be tenable for one year and shall be chargeable with a fee of Rs. 1/-. Every Panda shall be bound to have the license of his gumastas renewed every year.

6. The licenses granted to Pandas and gumastas of the 2 classes shall be respectively in the prescribed form.

7. An advisory committee consisting of some reputed persons shall be formed to help and cooperate with the district magistrate in the issue of these licenses.

8. All applications for licenses should be made to this Committee. The committee will consider these applications and if the applicant be found suitable forward it with their recommendation to the District Magistrate for granting a license. If they are of opinion that the applicant is not worthy of getting the license the committee will send back the application with their reasons to the District Magistrate.

9. When any Gumasta desires to leave his employer and get employed under someone else, he shall obtain a transfer certificate from his employer. If his employer refused to grant the certificate without reasonable cause he shall apply to the Committee who will enquire from his employer and recommend such action on his application as they think fit.

10. An officer of a rank equivalent to that of sub-Deputy Collector shall be employed by the District Magistrate to supervise and control the work.

11. It shall be duty of this officer as far as possible to meet all trains and see that no person acts as a Panda or as a *Gumasta* without a licence and that the licenced persons abide by the conditions of their license. He shall decide on the spot all disputes arising between rival Pandas and report all cases of misconduct on their part.

12. A Register giving details about all licensed Pandas and *Gumastas* shall be kept by this officer and all changes shall be noted therein.

The break out of Cholera was a regular feature in Puri due to unhygienic and insanitary conditions which were prevalent in the earlier days. The root cause of cholera was the eating of bad food. All the pilgrims consume mahaprasad when they are at Puri during festivities. Mahaprasad is good when fresh, but it becomes stale after some hours like all other types of cooked food.

In the report of the Pilgrim Committee the matter regarding the eating of *Mahaprasad* featured prominently. What the members observed in this regard are quoted below.

The distinctive feature of the pilgrimage to Puri is the Mahaprasad, the sacred food which has been consecrated by offering to the Lord Jagannath and other deities. The *Mahaprasad* is considered as sacred that all may eat this food together irrespective of caste distinctions. To eat the Mahaprasad is one of the chief rites of the pilgrimage and no pious Hindu in good health would think of cooking his own food while at Puri. The conditions under which this food is cooked and sold are obviously of great importance with reference to the public health. Sometimes the pilgrims do not get fresh *Mahaprasad* and has to eat stale stuff and this is the main reason for the out break of Cholera, diarrhoea and other enteric troubles. The committee recommended certain measures to be taken strictly so that pollution of food should be controlled and occurrence of epidemics would be minimised.

(a) The wells are insufficiently protected and at least one of them in the Ananda Bazar is much used by the pilgrims who come to eat the *Mahaprasad.* It would be a great improvement if these wells could all be covered over and have pumps attached. This we understand is impossible as there are very strong objections. We would recommend that the wells should have their cylinders thoroughly plastered with cement and that they should be provided with efficiently drained plinths, with parapets around their mouths and with pulleys, ropes and buckets for drawing water.

(b) The kitchens are good but the drains outside are defective and attract flies. Between the drains and the kitchen is a space which is much used as a urinal. It is important that there should be no stagnation in the drains as the sullage from the kitchen consists almost wholly of rice washings which decompose quickly. It was recommended that they should be constructed with glazed earthenware pipes laid in cement or of other impervious material such as Indian patent stone. They should also be placed close to the kitchen walls to avoid the intervening space being polluted.

(c) Near the kitchens are some houses for the cooks and other servants. The houses do not belong to the temple, but it would be an improvement if these are acquired and removed, new houses of a good pattern being built in their place. The area around these houses and between them and the kitchens might also be paved with advantage.

(d) Several areas within the temple are polluted and suitable steps should be taken to stop pollution.

4

Growth and Development of Puri

Offices, Institutions and Organizations both Governmental and Non-Governmental, Monasteries, Private organization, Educational Institutions of different sects, Akhada (Club house), Jegaghar, Hotel and lodging, Banks and Dharmasalas, Festivals and Sahis (streets) etc. are existing in Puri Town.

Government Offices-State Government and Central Government

- The Collectorate Office
- The Raj Bhavan (Residence of the Governors)
- The District Judge
- The District Industries Officer
- The Superintendent of Police
- The Marriage and Registration Office
- District Agriculture Officer
- Assistant Soil Conservation Officer
- The Executive Engineer, Rural Engineering Organisation

- The Executive Engineer, Puri Electrical Division.
- The Executive Engineer, Roads and Buildings.
- The Executive Engineer, Irrigation
- The Executive Engineer, Embankment and Drainage Division No. II
- The Commercial Tax Officer
- The Assistant Registrar, Co-operative Societies
- The Inspector of Schools
- The District Inspector of Schools
- The Chief District Medical officer.
- The Family Planning Officer
- The Additional Settlement Officer
- The Superintendent of Excise
- The Charge Officer, Settlement
- The Superintendent of Fisheries
- The Junior Employment Officer
- The District Statistical Officer
- The Forest Range Officer
- The Superintendent of Water Works
- The Tourist Information Officer
- The Magistrate, Lodging House Fund Committee
- The District Animal Husbandry and Veterinary Officer
- The Assistant Commissioner of Commercial Taxes.

- Criminal and the Civil Courts
- Post Office
- Circuit House
- Storm Signal Mast
- Meteorological Observatory
- Houses of District Officials
- South Eastern Railway, Hotel
- Public Works Departments
- Inspection Bungalow
- Forest rest House
- Puri Municipality
- The Superintendent of Post Offices
- The Field Publicity Officer
- The Deputy Account General (Works)
- The Income-tax Officer, Puri Circle
- Fire Station
- G.R.P
- Office of the Superintendent of Police
- Police Station
  - — Kumbharpada Thana
  - — Town Police Station
  - — Sidhamahavir Outpost
  - — Sinhadwara Police Station

- — Temple Outpost
- — Sadar Thana
- — Sea Beach Thana
- — Town Thana

Educational Institution

- Puri Zilla School
- Gadadhar High English School
- Biswambhar Vidyapitha
- Utkal Hindi Vidyapitha, Gundichamandir
- Government Girls' High School
- Markandeswar Sahi Girls' High School
- Swargadwara Girls' High School
- Gopabandhu Ayurvedic College
- The Superintendent of Sanskrit Studies, Orissa
- Shri Sadasiv Kendriya Sanskrit Vidyapeetha
- Samanta Chandra Sekhar College
- Mahila College
- Industrial Training Institute

Hospital, Dispensaries and Nursing Homes

- District H.Q. Hospital
- Infectious Disease Hospital Badasankha
- Gopabandhu Ayurveda Hospital
- Karmala Devi Maternity Home

- Sisu Bhawan (Childrens; Hospital)
- Sri Jagannath Yoga Chkichhalaya, Yoga Niketan
- Nilachal Nursing Home
- Sachi Health Clinic
- Bimala Health Centre
- Public Health Centre
- Blood Bank

Non Governmental Organizations

- Anchalika Mahila Vikas Kendra/AMVK
- ANKUR
- Bikramananda Institute for Rural Development/ BIRD
- Center For Educational and Social Development/ CESD
- Center for Organizational Research and Development/CORD
- All India Central Govt. Pensioners' Association
- All Orissa Traditional Taekwondo Association/ AOTTA
- Bright Association for Nobel and Decent Human Understanding/BANDHU
- Bureau of Education to Community Organization and National Crativity on Literature & Universal Brotherhood/BECONCLUB
- Community Development and Social Welfare Organization/CDSWO

- Indian Proctology Society/AYUS
- Indira Gandhi Mission-India/IGM-India
- Indradyumna Club
- Janamangal Samittee
- Jibaramjee Club
- Lingarajkala Niketan
- Mass Associatioin for Social Service/MASS
- Narayana-Annapurna Memorial Trust
- National Youth Organization/NYO
- Pargati
- Puri Seva Samiti
- Rajiv Gandhi Development Council for Rural Poor/RGDCRP
- Rural and Urban Socio Cultural Help/RUSH
- Sakhichand Bal-Niketan
- Sarbodaya Kalyan Samiti
- Social Workers' Organization for Rural Development/SWORD
- Sri Jagannath Samarkala Prasikhana Goveshna Pratisthan
- Sri Nrusingha Dev Anchalika Yuba Parisada/ SNDAYP
- Trisakti Arts Society/TAS
- United Seva Sangha/USS
- Yoga Niketana

Hotels and Lodgings

Athithi Hotel
Bagadia Dharmasala
Banga Laxmi Hotel
Bijay international Hotel
Bishnu Bhawan Hotel
Comfort Lodge
Dreak Land Cottage
Gandah Hotel
Golden palace Hotel
Railway guest House
Railway Hotel
Happy home Lodge
Heaven Hotel
Holiday inn Hotel
Holiday resort Hotel
Hotel anjana
Hotel basa
Hotel garden Resort,
Hotel Jyoti
Hotel Konark
Hotel lee Garden
Hotel Manisha
Hotel Padma
Hotel Prince
Hotel Roompam
Hotel Rupam
Hotel Samudra Pvt. Ltd.
Chakratitha Road
Hotel Sea Point Pvt. Ltd.
Hotel Subhdra
Hotel Swasti (P) Ltd.
Hotel Swosty (P) Ltd.
Hotel Vijaya (P) Ltd
Jagabalia Lodge
Laxmi Hotel
Lokanath Lodgeing
Kins Fisher Hotel
Mayfair Beach Resort
Mohini Lodge
New Grand Hotel
Nilachal Asok Hotel
Niladri Lodge
Nilachal Lodging
Nilachal Lodge
New Sea Hawk Hotel
New Victoria Club Hotel

Nilamadhab Hotel
OTDC Pantha Nivas
Ocean View Hotel
Park Beach Resort (P) Ltd.
Park Hotel
Prachi Hotel
Puri Hotel
Radha Ballava Lodge
Railway Hotel
Raj Hotel
Rani Hotel,
Renuka Lodge
Renuka Bhaban Lodge
Roy Sons Holiday Homes
Repose Hotel
Rohit Hotel
Rumani Hotel
Sagar Lodge
Sagarika Hotel
Sagarsaikat Lodge
Samundra Sundari Hotel
Samundra Hotel
Sankar International Hotel
Santana Lodge
Safari International Hotel
Sea Foam Hotel
Sea Gul Hotel
Sea King Hotel
Sea Pearl Hotel
Sea Qull Hotel
Sea View Hotel
Sonali Hotel
Surya Lodge
Tosali Sands Hotel
Tourist Home Hotel
Tow Lodge
Victoria Club Hotel
View Hotel
VIP Lodge
Z Hotel

It is stated that out of 752 Maths established through out India, Now 181 Maths continue to exist at Puri and some of the existing Mathas are listed below, giving their names and sects to which they belong.

Name of the Matha		*Type, Sect (Sampradaya)*
Abadhuta Matha	..	Modern
Arjunadas Math	..	Gouda Madhava
Achyuta Matha	..	Goudiya
Bada Santha	..	Ramanuj
Bada Matha	..	Khairata
Bada Akhada	..	Pancha Ramanandi
Bada Oriya	..	Ati Badi
Bauli Math	..	Nanakpanthi
Balaram Kota	..	Ramanandi
Bada Chhata	..	Ramanandi
Bada Jhadu	..	Angila
Balagandi Math	..	Ramanandi
Bada Bramhachari Matha	..	Gouda Madhava
Bali Babaji Matha	..	Gouda Madhava
Bankimuhan Matha alias Padmacharan Das Math	..	Atibadi
Bisakha Matha	..	Gauda Madhava
Bharati	..	Adwaita
Balabhadra Chhata	..	Madhwacharya
Chhauni	..	Ramanandi
Chaulia Matha	..	Gouda Madhava
Chikiti Matha	..	Nimbarka
Chakratirtha Matha alias Pandit Matha	..	Ramanuj
Sri Ram Das Matha	..	Ramanuj
Dasavatara Matha	..	Ramanandi
Dampara Matha	..	Gauda Madhava
Dagara Matha	..	Angila
Dukhishyam Baba Matha	..	Abadhuta
Emar Matha	..	Ramanuj
Falahari Matha	..	Abadhuta
Gangamata Matha	..	Goudiya
Gandharva Matha	..	Goudiya
Gopal Tirtha	..	Adwaita
Gour Kishore Jew Matha	..	Goudiya
Goswami Matha	..	Goudiya

(Contd.)

(Table Contd.)

Name of the Matha		Type, Sect (Sampradaya)
Ghumsar Matha	..	Ramanandi
Haladia Matha	..	Gouda Madhava
Haridas Thakur Matha	..	Goudiya
Hati Gurudeva Matha	..	Ananta Sampradaya
Hati Akhada Matha	..	Ramanandi
Haridakhandi matha	..	Ramanandi
Jagannathaballava	..	Vishnuswami
Jagannath alias Patitapaban Matha	..	Ramanandi
Jayapur Matha	..	Khairata
Jagata Mohini Matha	..	Ramanuj
Jatia Babaji Matha	..	Gouda Madhava
Jena Matha	..	Gouda Madhava
Jejeram Matha	..	Ramanandi
Jhanjapita	..	Goudiya
Jeer Swamy	..	Ramanuj
Jogada	..	Modern
Kabir Chaura	..	Kabirpanthi
Kalitilaka	..	Goudiya
Kadali Patuka	..	Angila
Kataki Matha	..	Ramanuj
Kanasa Matha	..	Gouda Madhava
Mrupa Samudra Matha	..	Gouda Madhava
Kausalya Das	..	Ramanuj
Kunja Matha	..	Goudiya
Kothabhoga	..	Goudiya
Labanikhia Matha	..	Angila
Languli Matha	..	Dasanami
Lunia Chowdhury	..	Goudiya
Mahiprakas	..	Brahmachari
Mangu	..	Nanakapanthi
Malei Matha	..	Angila
Mahaprabhujike Baithaka	..	Ballavakula
Mahibiria Matha	..	Ramanuja
Mani Rama Matha alias Kaopudia Matha	..	Ramanandi

(Contd.)

(Table Contd.)

Name of the Matha		*Type, Sect (Sampradaya)*
Nandini Matha	..	Goudiya
Naga Matha	..	Ramanandi
Narasinghachari Matha	..	Ramanuj
Nebal Das Matha	..	Ramanuj
Narayan Chhata Matha	..	Goudiya
Nirmohi Akhada	..	Pancha Ramanandi
Nua Matha	..	Ramanuj
Nima Akhada	..	Pancha Ramanandi
Nirbani Akhada	..	Rancha Ramanandi
Niranjana Chhata	..	Aghorapanthi
Nidhi Das Matha	..	Goudiya
Nandi Matha	..	Goudiya
Omkarnath Sitaram Das	..	Gouda Madhava
Paramananda Das	..	Gouda Madhava
Punjabi Matha	..	Ramanandi
Purana Sava Matha	..	Angila
Poda Matha	..	Angila
Pipalayana alias Papudia Matha	..	Ramanandi
Shri Purusottama Matha	..	Goudiya
Ramakrishna	..	Modern
Ramji Matha	..	Nimbarka
Radhavallavi	..	Noimbarka
Radhakanta	..	Madhwa Goudeswar
Raghab Das	..	Ramanuj
Ramanuja Kota	..	Ramanuj
Ranganaikachari	..	Ramanuj
Rima Chhatra	..	Khairata
Rani Matha	..	Khairata
Runi Matha	..	Goudiya
Ramakrishna Matha	..	Dashnami Sannyasi
Sankarananda	..	Dandi Sannyasi
Sankaracharya or Bhogabardhan	..	Dandi Sannyasi
Samadhi Matha	..	Ramanuj

(Contd.)

(Table Contd.)

Name of the Matha		*Type, Sect (Sampradaya)*
Sanachhata	..	Ramanuj
Sana Jhadu	..	Ramanuj
Satalahari	..	Ati Badi
Satasasan Giridharoi Matha	..	Ati Badi
Sisu Matha	..	Utkaliya Vaisnava
Siddha Matha	..	Ramanuj
Sitaram Kota	..	Ramanuj
Sidhabakula Matha	..	Goudiya
Sidha Bramhachari matha	..	Madhwacharya
Suna Goswami	..	Goudiya
Sundar Das	..	Pancha Ramanandi
Sivatirtha	..	Adwaita
Sana Oriya Matha	..	Ati Badi
Swargadwara Chhata	..	Ramanandi
Surangi Matha	..	Goudiya
Sana Tarala alias Radha Krishna Matha	..	Goudiya
Satyaprakas	..	Gadua madhava
Trimali	..	Ramanuj
Torani Chhatra Matha	..	Ramanandi
Tata Gopinatha matha	..	Goudiya
Uttara Parswa	..	Ramanuj
Vania Chhatra	..	Khairat
Venkatachari	..	Khairat

Name of the Ashram

- Angira Ashram
- Ginaribant Ashram
- Guru Nanak Ashram
- Jatiababa Ashram
- Kanchi Kamakoti Ashram

- Karamala Abhiram Paramahamsa Ashram
- Langulibaba Ashram
- Markanda Ashram
- Pandya Maharshi Ashram
- Vrugu Ashram

List of Sahis (Streets)

Seven Important Sahi and Minor Sahis

Main Sahis

(1) Dalikadevi Sahi

(2) Harachandi Sahi

(3) Markandeswar Sahi

(4) Kundheibenta Sahi

(5) Dolamandap Sahi

(6) Bali Sahi

(7) Goudabada Sahi

Minor Sahis

(8) Baddei Sahi

(9) Balagandi Sahi

(10) Baseli Sahi

(11) Ganamala Sahi

(12) Gudia Sahi

(13) Gurunti Sahi

(14) Haragouri Sahi

(15) Kalikadevi Sahi

(16) Karatia Sahi

(17) Kapalamochana Sahi

(18) Khatua Sahi

(19) Khuntia Sahi

(20) Kumuti Sahi

(21) Manikarnika Sahi

(22) Mausima Sahi

(23) Pathuria Sahi

(24) Patna Jenapur

(25) Patna Jagannathpur

(26) Patna Balabhadra Ballava

(27) Patna Malipada

(28) Patna Bali Sahi

(29) Patna Parrhee

(30) Patna Kumbhakarpara

(31) Patna Tikarapada

(32) Talichha Sahi

List of Akhadas (A Group of Club Houses) in Puri

(1) Bagha Akhada

(2) Bada Akhada

(3) Khaki Akhada

(4) Hati Akhada

(5) Nirmohi Akhada

(6) Nirvahi Akhada

(7) Balabhadra Akhada

(8) Uttarakali Akhada

(9) Pahara Akhada

Important Jegaghara (Gymnastic-cum-Club House) of Puri Town

(1) Marichakot Jaga

(2) Ganesh Guruja

(3) Kadambagarh Brahmi Jaga

(4) Gurujang

(5) Nuagarh

(6) Sankat

(7) Majena

(8) Mala

(9) Satabakhara

(10) Sundara

(11) Mali

(12) Bisuni

(13) Panda

(14) Bhoga

(15) Duari

(16) Gopaltirtha

(17) Panchuati

(18) Nuagarh

(19) Champagarh

(20) Khuntia

(21) Tapang

(22) Barabati

List of Festivals in Puri

(1) Snana Yatra

(2) Anasara, Maha Anasara or Navakalevara

(3) Nabayauvana and Netrotsaba

(4) Ratha Yatra

(5) Herapanchami

(6) Gundicha Ghar Navadina Yatra

(7) Sayana Ekadashi

(8) Garuda Sayana Dwadashi

(9) Karkata Sankranti or Dakhinayan Yatra

(10) Chitalagi Amabasya

(11) Jhulana Yatra

(12) Gamhapurnima or Balabhadra Janma

(13) Rahurekha Lagi

(14) Krishna Janma

(15) Krishna Lila

(16) Satpuri Amabasya

(17) Ganesh Chaturthi

(18) Rekha Panchami or Risi Panchami

(19) Radhastami

(20) Parsvaparibartana

(21) Baman Janma or Sunia

(22) Ananta Chaturdashi

(23) Indra-Govinda Puja

(24) Dwitiya Osha

(25) Dasahara

(26) Kumar Purnima

(27) Hari Uthapana Ekadashi

(28) Garuda uthapan Dwadashi

(29) Navanna or Partaking of new rice

(30) Prathamastami

(31) Odhan Sasti

(32) Bakul Amabasya

(33) Pusyabhiseka

(34) Uttarayan Yatra

(35) Basanta Panchami

(36) Magha Purnima

(37) Siva Ratri

(38) Benta or Sikar

(39) Dola Yatra

(40) Chaitra Gundicha

(41) Ashokstami

(42) Rama Navami

(43) Damanaka Chori, Dayanalagi

(44) Pana Sankaranti or Mahabishuba Sankaranti

(45) Chandan Yatra

(46) Niladri Mahodays

(47) Nrusingha Janma

(48) Shital Sasthi

(49) Rajendraviseka

(50) Rukmini Harana

List of Banks Existing in Puri Town

- Puri Nimapara Cooperative Bank
- Puri Urban Cooperative Bank
- State Bank of India
- Punjab National Bank
- Allahabad Bank
- Andhra Bank

- Uco Bank
- Syndicate Bank
- Bank of Boroda
- Puri Gramya Bank
- Indian bank

List of Dharmasalas Existing in Puri Town

1. Goenika Dharmasala
2. Duduwala Dharmasala
3. Bagadia Dharmasala
4. Kanyalal Dharmasala
5. Khemka Dharmasala
6. Dhanjee Magi Dharmasala

5

Guardians of Sacred Complex and Continuity in Sacred Tradition

The structure and organization of the Sacred Tradition is preserved and maintained by certain guardians and cultural specialists. This does not mean that the sacred system is free from change. Various forces such as the changing political order and administrative setup, economic strain and social modernization try to induce change in the system. But the guardians of the tradition and various control mechanisms keep the forces of change in check and inhibit basic structural change in the tradition.

There are eight important guardians of the cultural traditions and Sacred Complex of Puri:

(1) The Gajapati Rajas of Orissa

(2) The ritual specialists and functionaries (Sebaka) Sanskrit Pandits, and Brahmin Pandits.

(3) The ascetics and the monastic order (Mathas)

(4) The cultural centres of Puri (Parab Jatras, Akhada and Jegaghars, Sahi Jatra)

(5) The Sasan Villages, Muktimandapa and Pandits.

(6) The Minor Rajas of Feudatory States.

The Gajapati Rajas of Orissa

The Gajapati Rajas are the paramount guardians of the tradition. They are the founders, patrons, and saviours of the tradition.

The core of the tradition is Lord Jagannath, the paramount deity of Orissa and the Gajapati Rajas of Orissa and the foremost Sebaks and worshippers of the deity. They have donated vast wealth in cash and kind to the Jagannath temple for the Seba Puja of the deity. They have associated themselves intimately with all kinds of activities, secular and religious concerning, the deity, and, therefore, the public considers the Gajapati Rajas the mobile form of the Lord Jagannath.

Out of the public image have grown many myths and symbols which reinforce the relationship that exists between the paramount deity and the paramount Rajas of Orissa. These mythic and ritualistic relationships are responsible for preserving the Sacred Tradition largely intact.

Because of this intimate association between them, there exist many similarities between the palace of the Gajapati Rajas (*Srinahara*) and the temple of Lord Jagannath (Srimandir). One of the important physical similarities is the lion's gate, which is present in front of the palace and the temple. The special privilege of having the lion's gate is exclusive to Lord Jagannath and the Gajapati King of Orissa.

The significance of the Gajapati Raja of Orissa as the guardian of the sacred tradition is expressed in the analysis of the temple rituals of the Raja at the Lord

Jagannath Temple. The Gajapati Raja as the foremost Sebak enjoys privileges of offering special services such as sweeping the three cars with a golden broom (*Chera Panhara*) at the time of the car festival, There are several other ritualistic privileges which are enjoyed exclusively by the Gajapati Raja. No one else dare claim them for fear of penalty of death or disease.

One of the significant ritual performances which is observed by the Raja every morning in the palace shows a close association between the Raja and Lord Jagannath. This ritual is called *Debarchan* (Worshipping God). After morning ablutions (*abakash*) of Lord Jagannath are over at the temple the tooth stick which is used to brush the teeth of Lord Jagannath, a little of water in which the Lord is bathed and the coconuts which are offered to the Lord at the time of the Lord's slumber at night are carried by special temple Sebaks to the palace. The Raja's morning ablutions are performed with the Lord's tooth stick water, etc. in exactly the same manner as in the case of the Lord. The Raja sits on a wooden seat in the room where the Debarchan is performed, Rajaguru (the priest of the palace) perform the rituals. In fact, the Raja's teeth and brushed in the same mock manner as in the case of Lord Jagannath. Because of his intimate ritual association with Lord Jagannath the Raja is regarded as the God-King and mobile Vishnu. This very association between Lord Jagannath and the Gajapati Raja who is the guardian of the temple organization helps considerably to preserve and maintain the Sacred Complex and the cultural traditions linked with it.

Besides being the chief ritual functionaries of the temple and the spiritual lord of their kingdom, the Gajapati Rajas were in charge of the temple estate and endowments. They used to keep an account of the income and expenditure of the temple and render them at the Jameswar Siva temple, to the Deputy of the Lord

Jagannath at a special religious ceremony held for this purpose on the full moon day of the month of July August.

The most important function of the Gajapati Rajas as guardians of the Sacred Tradition is their control of all categories of Sebaks and supervision of their rituals and services in the temple. After shifting their capital from Khurda to Puri in 1817 they were in a better position to give their personal attention to the administration of the temple affairs. They used to go to the temple almost daily, sit for some hours in a place called *Beharan Pinda* (watching spot) and watch the activities and the duties of the Sebaks. When the affairs of the temple were under the immediate control and management of the Gajapati Rajas they had the power of taking firm action against the Sebaks for any neglect of the ritual services and infringement of the temple rules. The Rajas were also entitled to punish the Sebaks with fines or corporal chastisement even for the slightest deviation from the prescribed hourly duties and performance of the festivities.

There are ancient books (Pothis, either of palm-leaves or of paper) which contain the minutest particulars regarding Lord Jagannath and the proper modes of carrying on the rites and ceremonies in the temple, and the bad omens that can possibly occur and the modes of averting them. One such written record is Niladri Mohodaya which serves as a scriptural reference on the rituals and services offered to the Lord Jagannath and the measures adopted in the temple on the appearance of bad omens.

The temple scribe (*Deul Karana*) and accountant of the temple is in charge of a bundle of palm-leaves (*Karmani*) in which are mentioned in detail the duties of the Sebaks of every description. In a separate section which follows we have given a detailed account of the ritual functionaries and the role they play in perpetuating the Sacred Complex connected with the temple of Lord Jagannath.

But at this stage two important matters concerning the performance of the ritual services and festivals by the ritual functionaries and the control and supervision of them by the administrative staff emerge from the study of the temple organization. We have given below a short account of the supervisory arrangement, which was set up by the Gajapati Rajas to meet these requirements.

The Gajapati Rajas set up proper administrative machinery to control the functionaries and ensure orderly and timely performance of the rituals and services in the temple and maintenance of the Sacred Complex.

The Gajapati Rajas appointed four officers called *Parichhas* to manage the estates and endowments of the temple and supervise the duties of the Sebaks for their due and regular duties and performance of the ritual service. All Sebaks worked in obedience to the instructions and orders of the Deul Parichha who was in charge of the management of the temple. He was authorized to (1) supervise the hourly rituals round the day and seasonal festivals round the year (2) inflict suitable punishments which were specified for different categories of Sebaks in case of neglect in and irregular attendance to their duties; and (3) prevent summoning any of the servants of the temple to the courts of Justice for trifling disputes amongst themselves.

The Parichhas were authorized by the Gajapati Rajas to enquire into the settle the disputes according to ancient usage and custom of the temple, but should any of them be guilty of any offence of any enormity then the Deul Parichha sent them to the magistrate and appointed another person to discharge their duties during their absence.

It is customary for the Sebaks whose appointments are hereditary to mortgage or sell their *chulis* or ovens and *pantis* or places where the pots are kept after cooking. On this account frequent disputes arise between the heirs of the Sebaks and the mortgagees or purchasers of the chulis and pantis. The disputes are decided by the Deul Parichha and a Council of Abbots (*Sanyasis*) and Brahmin Pandits and Celibates (*Brahmacharies*) who assemble for this purpose by the order of the Rajas. Their decision is final.

Filling up the situations of Sebaks when one becomes vacant by death without issue was the responsibility of the Rajas. The Deul Parichha and the principal Sebaks shall fix upon a successor and after an enquiry into the person's character and capabilities the Deul Parichha submits the report to the Rajas for their final decision in this matter.

The Sebaks obey the orders of Parichhas and in case of disobedience they are liable to be punished. The mode of punishment is different for different categories of Sebaks. The former Government punished the Sebaks by putting peons over the offenders and depriving them of their sacred food for a day or two in order to bring the Sebaks back to regular performance of their respective duties.

For the offences of untimely performance of the hourly rituals round the day, Mudiratha, Daitapati, Talluchha, Bhitarachha, and Chhatisha Nijoga Naik are fined three days Khei. (The Bhog or sacred food is divided amongst the Sebaks, The Gajapati Raja, the Mathadharies and others who are connected with the ritual services in the temple. Each Sebak receives a portion of the sacred food being the remuneration paid for the services he renders in the temple. This portion of the sacred food is called Khei). In cases of repetition of the offence, they are fined in cash not exceeding five rupees, and for offences more grievous than these they may be dismissed from their respective offices unless they can assign good and sufficient reason approved of by the Deul Parichha for their non-attendance.

For the similar offences the Pratihari, Suar and Panti Badu Sebaks are fined three days Khei and receive corporal punishment not exceeding 10 rottons (lashes). Such of the Sebaks as do not receive any Khei are fined in cash and receive corporal punishment not exceeding 10 rottons. They are also liable to be dismissed for offences of greater enormity. If the *Akhanda Mekapa* or the Sebak in charge of lighting the temple is negligent in his duties he is fined in cash and also receives corporal punishment. The Parichha is particularly careful that this service be duly and properly performed and in case of disobedience of his orders in this matter the Sebak of this category is liable to severe punishment.

The Gajapati Rajas had power to boycott any Sebak for offences committed by him of stealing consecrated food or any other temple property and of telling lies and misbehaving with other Sebaks. The punishment of boycott, which is known as *Basanda*, is of two types-Seba Basanda, prevention from performing the ritual services, and Deul Basanda, for bidding entry to the temple.

To illustrate, we furnish below a few typical cases relating to the types of punishment given by Gajapati Raja Vira Kesari Deb (A.D. 1737-1773) for offences of lying and of stealing temple property or consecrated food from the Kitchen. Of the entire Gajapati Raja Vira Kesari Deb reigned for a long period of 51 years, under the suzerainty of the Marathas.

The letters sent by Gajapati Vira Kesari Deb from his palace in Khurda to the Supervisor (Parichha) of the temple and other subordinate officials are reproduced below.

Letter No.1
Sri Purusottama's Great Temple

Sri Vira Kesari Deb, 9th regnal year (Anka), Taurus, 20th day.

Acknowledge the receipt of the letter from Parichha of the Western Gate. The Ghatuara in charge of swimming the deity in water and Rama Mahapatra, the holder of the Flat Umbrella, beat a man with the handle of the umbrella and by so doing broke the handle into two pieces. Why did he use the handle of the umbrella for beating? He is to be blamed. When the Great God (*Sri Thakura* here refers to the King as God) will come to Puri, punishment will be meted out to the accused.

Letter No. 2
Sri Purusottama's Great Temple

Sri Vira Kesari Deb, 14th regnal year, Scorpio, 10th day

The following temple functionaries of the category of cook (suara) in charge of the King's endowed share of food gifts (*kotha bhoga)*-Bika Mahanti, Badu laichhana *Mahasuara*, and Baban Mahasuara, watchman Narana Mahasuara, while they were on duty, kept hidden pieces of cakes prepared for offering to the Deity in an earthen cover (tetauni), and finished the middle offerings. Narana Mahasuara came and closed the doors. There was 1 half hours of day left before sunset when his son Baban Mahasuara came and opened the door and did his work. He then reported that there was a shortage of 9 cakes. This matter was placed before the Abbot Astagrasi Gosain (who looks to the performance of ritual services at the temple). The functionaries on duty said that as the cakes had been improperly cooked, so they had been thrown into the oven. Required quantities of food materials were given and they were used in preparing the consecrated food.

Narana Mahasuara, son of Paramananda Mahasuara remains boycotted (basanda). The watchman Dania Mahasuara is also boycotted.

Letter No. 3
Sri Purusottama's Great Temple

Sri Vira Kesari Deb, 25th regnal year, Cancer, 12th day.

This is in respect of offences committed by the temple functionaries. The oven in the temple kitchen of Rama Mishra's monastery was dirty. All the food materials supplied for the preparation of consecrated food were stolen and Krupasindhu Panda (a functionary of the Dhopakhal category) and Madhab Panda (a functionary of the Angarua duty. Collect a fine of 40 Kahanas (1 kahana=1280 cowries) from each of them.

Letter No. 4
Sri Vira Kesari Deb, 34 regnal year, Aquarius, 12th day

The order of Gajapati Vira Kesari is submitted below.

The Astrologer reported the case of the theft of the head ornament. He said that Krushna Pasupalaka had stolen it.

I asked Krushna Pasupalaka to undergo an ordeal by holding a hot ball (uanda) in his hand. He held it, but it did not fall down. So I order that you give him cloth and sandal from the temple and restore him in the service of Garabadu.

(This last case which follows is not a letter from the King but an agreement reached by a group of temple functionaries of the Pharaka category regarding the distribution of largesse among coparceners and in case of violation of agreement by any cosharer as to what sort of punishment should be meted out to the transgressor).

The Abbot Paramahansa Astagrasi Gosain, helped a group of the temple functionaries of the Pharaka confederacy (Nijoga) to come to an agreement among themselves regarding the distribution of receipts from pilgrims. The agreement is as follows.

Letter No. 5
Vira Kesari Deb, 4th regnal year, Capricornus, 17th day

When the pilgrims will come we all of the Pharaka confederacy will sit down and choose one according to our consent and put him as a guide in charge of the pilgrims, and whatever we earn from this we will share and enjoy. When the Khandayat comes for a view of God (darsana), likewise whatever Paiks (militia of the State) donate to our confederacy and whatever our patrons (*Jajamanas*) and also Bengali Paikars donate when they come for a visit of the God; whatever we receive from the Jagamohan estate (Jagamohan is a building inside the temple where the pilgrims offer their presents) and from the Lion's Gate, and whatever presents we receive from our pilgrims; whatever income we obtain from all these sources, whether it is gain or loss, we will distribute equally among all the members now forming our confederacy. In case there is any amount to be paid we all will pay that sum in equal proportion.

Here we eleven of the Pharaka confederacy put our signatures below.

Lava Muduli, Rath Muduli, Anama Muduli, Govinda Muduli, Hadu Muduli, Nailai Muduli, Phula Muduli, Rama Muduli, Chakala Muduli Madhab Muduli, Bihari Daraga.

Whoever among us acts against what has been stated above, shall be fined 100 kucha (1 kucha = 320 tolas) of ghee and this will be donated to kotha bhoga. He will also be kept out of the temple. We are agreeable to all this.

The administration of the Jagannath temple has changed hands, sometimes resting with the new rulers, at others resting with the Gajapati Rajas who were treated as the Superintendent of the temple. The temple and the Sacred Complex associated with it flourished under the royal patronage of the independent Gajapati Rajas of Orissa. But when the glory of the empire of the Hindu rulers was lost the sacred institutions and the cultural traditions suffered a serious set back as a result of the disastrous attacks on Puri and other cultural centres by the Muslim and Moghul rulers. But in spite of their invasion and depredation the temple organization continued almost with the same name and fame as before.

When Orissa came under the rule of the Marhattas from 1756 to 1803 the situation in the management of the temple was improved. Being Hindus, the Marhattas encouraged the worship and got the ceremonies and festivals properly done. The same respect and honour was shown to it by the British when they took possession of Puri and the Jagannath temple in 1803. We have already quoted earlier what instructions British authorities issued to their troops in this regard and how they should treat the temple and the functionaries upon their arrival at Puri.

For the first few years the British like the Marhattas managed the temple and its estates and endowments direct and as pointed out earlier had annually made up the difference between the receipts and the expenditure of the temple.

The Ritual Specialists and Functionaries (Sebaka) Sanskrit Pandits, and Brahmin Pandits

The ritual services of the temple of Lord Jagannath are well defined, fixed and multiplex. To perform these services vast multitude of ritual functionaries Sebaks are appointed whose duties, rights, and liabilities are codified in a palm-leaf document called the Karmani. To check irregularities in the services and conflicts among the Sebaks the Government passed the Act XIV of 1952 (Puri Shri Jagannath Temple (Administration) Act, 1952) to prepare a Record-of-Rights consolidating the rights and duties of the Sebaks and the emoluments, which they are entitled to. The Record-of-Rights which is the legalized document of Karmani help in determining the roles played by the Sebaks in the Sibapuja of the temple and in deciding disputes arising among them and the emoluments they are entitled to for the services rendered by them in the temple.

In former times the establishment of the temple of Lord Jagannath consisted only of a few Sebaks because the ritual services were of a limited number, Mr. C. Grome, who was the Collector of the Puri district in 1805 has mentioned in his report to the Secretary to the Commissioner of Cuttack that there were in the past 36 types of Sebaks and they were in consequence called Chhatisia Nijoga. In course of time, the Gajapati Rajas, Princes, public and pilgrims, made more endowments to the temple, which was necessitated by the greater elaboration of the ritual services and worship of the deities in the temple. To perform them were needed a greater number of Sebaks and a division of labour among them. Mr. Grome stated in his report inter alia, "From a period of at least 200 years others have been added to these original 36 Sebaks and the number now belonging to the temple amounts to 250." Shri L. Panda has mentioned in his report, There are more than 140 kinds of Sebaks and besides, these Sebaks, here are various other institutions and individuals connected with the Seba Puja. In fact the Record-of-Rights which he prepared includes 119 categories of Sebaks.

To the public the Sebaks are known as pandas, a generic term used for the constellation of the Sebaks. But in reality the pandas are those who are concerned with the pilgrims. They are called Jatri Panda (Pilgrim Panda) and the considered to be tirthaguru.

The important duty of the Pandas is to visit different parts of India, preach the philosophy and doctrine of Jagannath cult among the Hindus, collect pilgrims and escort them to Puri. They are also responsible for providing lodging and boarding to them in dharmasalas at Puri and arrange a darsan of Lord Jagannath for them and a visit to different sacred centres and tirthas located in the town and in its vicinity.

In the past the pilgrims were delivered over to the pandas and their agents at various check-posts at the entrance gates on the routes leading to Puri. The Pandas maintained a list of the pilgrims who were in their charge and whom they escorted to Puri on pilgrimage. This arrangement was necessary for the collection of pilgrim tax from them. Any panda who tried to hide any pilgrim with the intention of evading payment of the pilgrim tax was severely punished. The Collector of Tax at Jagannath used to issue to the pilgrims licence of access to the temple and perform the customary ceremonies under the charge of their respective pandas. At the expiration of the period mentioned in the licence the pandas were responsible to collect these licences from the pilgrims under their charge and return them to the Collector of Tax, in default where of the pandas or their agents were subject to such fine as was considered proper in the circumstances of the case.

There were two reasons for making the pilgrims over to the pandas: first, to prevent unnecessary delays at the chowkies or passes and second, to prevent people of low caste going into the temple since pandas were answerable for offences of this nature.

When there was no railway and vehicular conveyance to Puri the pandas used to go on foot to different parts of India to meet those of their patrons (Jajamans) who had visited Puri once or twice on pilgrimage and establish contacts with new patrons and indoctrinate them with the Jagannath Dharma. The pandas were may say are solely responsible for making Puri known to the people all over India and spreading the Jagannath Dharma far and wide. When they make their journey they carry with them sufficient quantities of consecrated food for distributing among the devotees of Lord Jagannath. The faith and devotion to Lord Jagannath are so firm and deep seated that as soon as a man of any village in a far-off place meets someone coming from Puri town he is overwhelmed in Bhakti towards Lord Jagannath and feels himself as if he were in the pilgrim centre and lies down prostrate on the ground.

I have witnessed this in a garden of the Indian Institute of Advanced Study, Simla. While I was once taking a stroll in the apple garden of the Institute I came across the gardener who kept watch on the trees. We sat down together under an apple tree to chat. When he came to know that I was from Puri he solemnly folded his hands and bent down to touch the ground with his head and then stretch himself with his face downward. I was curious to find out why he had prostrated himself. He replied, "Seeing you or any man from Jagannath Puri is as sacred as seeing the Lord Himself. Many a time the Tirthagurus of Pandas have come to my village and many people have accompanied them to Puri on pilgrimage. But I have not yet had the chance to make a trip to the sacred centre. Nor do I hope to do it ever in my lifetime. Therefore, seeing you or a man of Jagannath dham I feel that I have attained some religious virtue and merit".

During their visit to different parts of the country the pandas receive grants of land and other properties from the well-to-do devotees for the express purposes of defraying the established expenses of the temple. The lands granted to Lord Jagannath for this purpose are known as *Amruta Manohi* which means that the produce from such lands is used for the purpose of offering Bhog independent of Kottabhog, that is, what is permanently allowed by the Government. Thousands of acres of Amruta Manohi land granted as khairata by numberless devotees belonging to different parts of the country are under the charge of the pandas and heads of the monasteries situated in Puri. They furnish the temple with articles and appropriate the proceeds of the lands for the purposes for which they were assigned and in keeping with the intention of the donors. Essentially the pandas have established in perpetuity the sacred link and a network of relationship between the public and the Sacred Complex.

As indicated earlier there is a vast multitude of Sebaks attending to the ritual services in the temple. One thing, which strikes us, is that even though the Sebaks belong to different castes, high and low, they are all considered equal in the eyes of Lord Jagannath and they are all his Sebaks. As a matter of fact no hierarchy is maintained among them as the duties and functions of all the Sebaks are equally important and all the Sebaks are interdependent and tied up together by a network of ritual and social relationships. Different functionaries perform different functions and by the very nature of their duties and rights some have control over others. But being founders of the temple and supreme guardians of the sacred tradition the Gajapati Rajas are not only the chief administrators and superintendents of the temple but also the foremost Sebaks of Lord Jagannath. Being the head of the temple they are the controlling authority of the Sebaks and have the power to punish them for any negligence in their ritual services by putting peons over the offenders and depriving them of their sacred food (Khei) and also dismissing them from their service. As superintendents they are in entire charge of the temple, and its internal management, its police and sanitary arrangements. They exercise the powers of issuing orders in matters of succession to any seba and sanction new appointments to the temple services. They are in charge of all immovable properties and the Ratna Bhandar of Lord Jagannath which consists of most valuable jewellery precious stones and gold ornaments. They are also in charge of all the temple funds and the liable as trustees to keep full accounts of the yearly income and expenditure of Lord Jagannath and His property.

Quite apart from this capacity as superintendent and trustee, the Gajapati Rajas as successors to the independent Kings of Orissa, have got certain important Sebas in the temple and also enjoy unique privileges for themselves and their family members including daily Kheis of consecrated food.

They are described in the Madala Panji as the Adya Sebak or the foremost Sebak with their duty of performing their ritual sweeping of the three cars with the golden broomstick during the car festival. They are entitled to a certain amount of consecrated food) Tat) on special occasions, and there are Sebaks specially deputed to carry this Tat to their palace accompanied by an elaborate ceremony. They are respected by the people as mobile Vishnu (Chalanti Vishnu) because whenever they go to the temple they are served in a manner next only to the Jagannath.

A list of other important Sebaks is given below indicating in brief the important duties and rituals, which they perform in the temple.

(1) *Mudirasta* : He officiates for the Raja in Cherapahara and other functions in case the Raja is prevented from performing them for one reason or another.

(2) *Chhatisha Nijoga Nayak Patjoshi Mahapatra and Bhandar Nayak* : He had vast powers and functions in the past but many of them are at present not in vogue. He comes from the Pusupalak class and till 1930 had the key of the Bhandar. He is to execute all orders of the Temple authorities and to see that all the Sebaks do their duty properly. He also performs the Sadi Bandha ceremony.

(3) *Bhitarch Mahapatra* : He is the first man to go for the Dwarfita (to open the door) ceremony and to examine the seals and has to perform the Sadi Bandha ceremony and check the purity of the Bhog offered.

(4) *Talich Mahapatra* : He seals doors at night pahur and controls and checks the purity of the kitchen.

(5) *Bhandar Mekap* : In charge of Bahar Bhandar containing all the jewellery required for the daily use of the deities.

(6) *Parichhas :* Parichhas were at one time managing the Temple. Their work has now been reduced to holding a gold cane at the Sankal Dhup Patuar (offering made in the morning) and during certain festivals.

(7) *Padhiaris* : Who guard the deities, go to call for Bhogs and are responsible for the safety of the pilgrims.

(8) *Gochikars* : These belong to the Padhiari class and watch the door called the Jay-Bijaya Dwar.

(9) *Binakar* : He plays the bind (lute) to the deities before he goes to sleep.

(10) *Bhitar Gayeni* sings songs at the time of Pahur (slumber) and at other festivals.

(11) *Samprada Nijog*, i.e., dancing girls who dance at the time of the Patuar (procession).

(12) *Madeli* plays the Madal (drum) at the time of the Patuar.

(13) *Sankhua* plays the sankh (conch) with the Baijayantries (musicians).

(14) *Kahalia* : Blows Bije Kahali (bungle).

(15) *Ghantua* and Ghant Nijog work with bells daily and on festivals.

(16) *Amonia Chatar* : The chatar (an umbrella), the Taras (the flat umbrella), the kalakanti (a kind of umbrella)-sebaks for carrying umbrellas at festivals, etc.

(17) *Gitagovinda Sebak* : He recites the Gitagovinda before the Lord at Chandan Lagi (anointment of sandal).

(18) *Chakra Dihuri* and *Chamu Dihuri* carry masals (torches) at festivals, etc.

(19) The *Sinharis* or *Pasupalaks* dress the Lords and put flowers on him at all times and do the Abakash (Paja (morning rituals).

(20) *Suar Badhus* (*Bhog Saita Suar Badu, Behera Suar Badu*) : These wash the Pokharia (the place in front of the lion's platform where food is offered) several times.

(21) *Patri Badu*: supplies the *Puja Upakarans* (ingredients of worship) throughout the day.

(22) *Gara Badu* : He serves the gods by supplying water at the time of Pujas and other *Nitis.*

(23) *Sudha Suara* and *Ansar Sudha Suara* : make preparations for Puja.

(24) *Muduli* : The incharge of Puja utensils and other daily *Puja Upakarans* and supplies to *Mekaps.*

(25) *Hadap Nayak, Bidia Jognia* and *Tambul Sebak* serve to prepare and carry betel leaves to the Lords.

(26) *Ghatuaris* prepare and serve *Ainla* (trifala), *Chandan* (sandal) and *Mahadipa* (great lamp) for the daily nitis and for the Parbajatra Nitis.

(27) Tulasia supplies *tulsi* leaves daily.

(28) *Dayanamalis* supplies daily scented flowers.

(29) *Mahabhoi* supplies curd and other milk products.

(30) *Pani-apat* supplies water required in the Temple throughout the day.

(31) *Balita Sebak* supplies *Arati Balita* (the wick used for ceremonial lamp).

(32) *Kumbhar Bishois* supplies Handi and Kudua (earthen pots) and other pottery required daily.

(33) *Daudia* supplies rope to draw water from the Shri Bimala well.

(34) *Malchul Sebak* supplies *Chul* (tuft of flower), etc., for some festivals.

(35) *Mulia Suansia* supplies *Kath Pidha* (fuel), etc.

(36) *Joganias* for Koth Bhog, Parbajatra, Ballav and Bahar Deuli to carry articles and Ballav (sweetmeat) and supply at required places.

(37) *Biman Badus* carry all Bije Bimans (a kind of carriage).

(38) *Chap Behera* and *Dalais* Work to prepare chaps (the float).

(39) *Rath Bhois* works and supplies labourers for construction of Cars.

(40) *Kalabethias* drag the Cars.

(41) *Karatias* or *Sawers* work on construction of the Cars.

(42) *Tamra Bishoi* works as a coppersmith during the Car festivals.

(43) *Chitrakars* and *Rupkars* (painter) colour and prepare the *Pratimas* (images) for decoration of the Cars. Ramesh Ch. Maharana, Bhubaneswar Mahapatra, Kulamani Maharani are the famous painters at Puri. Raghurajpur village is famous for painting.

(44) *Ojha Maharana* works as blacksmith

(45) *Rath Dahuk* sings on the Cars.

(46) *Banua* supplies fireworks when required.

(47) *Chaka Apsar* Sebak keeps charge from tailors.

(48) *Mandnities* Chandua (canopy) when required.

(49) *Koth Suansia* work as labourers to prepare huts, *chamundias* (leafy shed) etc. at festivals.

(50) *Suna Goswami* draws water from *Suna Kuan* (well) on *Snan Purnima* (bathing ceremony)

(51) *Darjis* stitch clothes, *Chaka Apsar* (pillows) etc.

(52) *Patras* prepares silk ropes, etc.

(53) *Badhais* or carpenters work on Cars and *Chaps*.

(54) *Panikund Sebak*, *Lugadhua* and *Mahasethi* work to wash the deities clothes.

(55) *Bania* prepares and repairs ornaments.

(56) *Mukha Pakhala* makes tooth-sticks for the deities.

(57) *Khatuli Sebak* puts *Khatuli* for Abakash Puja.

(58) *Darpania* supplies *Darpana* and also cleans the deities's utensils.

(59) *Baidya* or doctor gives medicine at *Anabasara* to the Lord. Late Maguni Brahma, Prafulla Panda, Purnachandra Rath, Govind Tripathy Lokanath Mishra, Narasingha Mohapatra these persons are famous for Ayurvedic.

(60) *Chunras* serve Garud.

(61) *Lenka* works to call the *Sebaks*.

(62) *Pradhani* works to call the *pandas* and has other duties. He distributes *Kheis* at the Mukti Mandap.

(63) *Paiks*, with their heads *Dolei* and *Dalbeheras*, stay throughout the day and night and work according to the orders of the temple authorities.

(64) Temple's Police guard the Temple.

(65) The *Mahasuaras* are the first to take the *Chheka* (food arranged for the offering) to the *Panti* (the place where the food is offered).

(66) *Suars* are of various kinds known by different names according to the nature of duties; those who cook and prepare Bhog like Badu Suar, Pitha Suar, Tuna Suar, Thai Suar, Amalu Suar, Bindua, Pagua, Amalu Toli, Tola Badu, and Tola Bati (who shows light).

(67) *Rosh Amin* and *Rosh Paika* watch and supervise the kitchen.

(68) *Handi Jogania* Supplies pots for Bhogs.

(69) *Bahar Deuli Suars* cooks in Shri Laxmi's Rosh.

(70) *Rosh Koth Bhog Pania* supplies water to the kitchen.

(71) *Paniki Pata* cuts and dresses vegetables.

(72) *Rosh Nikap* prepares Gandhan ingredients like ginger and distributes ghee to some Sebaks.

(73) Chaul Bacha cleans the rice to be cooked.

(74) *Chunamunda Samartha*, *Birimung Samartha* and *Biribuha Samartha* are those who supply rice, flour, and ground black gram.

(75) *Panti Badus* carries chhecks.

(76) *Biduas* make Muthmal or Chhecks ready.

(77) *Dho-Pakhalia*, *Gobar-Pania*, *Angarua* and *Rabadia* wash and clean the kitchen and *chulis* (ovens) and supply water for the purpose.

(78) *Sabut Nijog* has *Seba* on *Amabasya* days at Swargadwara.

(79) *Bentbindha Paik* has *Seba* on festive *Nitis*.

(80) *Mudra* puts Mudra at the time the seal is to be affixed.

(81) *Jyotisa* (Astrologer) astrological calculations and forecasting. Lokanath Mahapatra, Bamana Khadiratna are famous as astrologer.

Besides, the *Maths* or monastic houses in the town have each some ritual functions or the other to do in the temple.

The Ascetics and the Monastic Order (Mathas)

No account of the Sri Kshetra can be complete without some account of the monasteries or monastic houses called *Maths*. These Maths were founded in Puri by the religious teachers and preachers with the object of preaching for their respective religious sects, and spreading their particular philosophical doctrines, giving religious instructions to the disciples and generally encouraging a religious life, perpetuating the Guru Chela (spiritual guide-disciple) tradition and institutionalizing it by establishing religious centres and procedures of prayer and worship-dedicating their ritual services to Lord Jagannath and safeguarding the Jagannath cult and cultural institutions, and last but not least arranging feeding travellers, beggars, and ascetics.

The monasteries are intimately associated with the temple of Lord Jagannath in performing various religious duties such as in the case of the Uttarparswa Math, supplying special offerings of food, or as in the case of the Jagannath Ballava, providing flowers for the decoration of the deities or as in the case of the Jhanjapita Math, waking up the deities in the morning by playing on musical instruments, or sweeping and cleaning the temple precincts as in the case of Jhadu math. In emergencies the temple authorities consult the Mahants of the Maths and according to their advice solve many ritual problems. To illustrate, when a large piece of stone fell down from the ceiling of the temple, the authorities convened a meeting of the Mahants, discussed with them regarding the manner in which the temple could be repaired. On certain occasions the Government appoints the Mahanta of Emar Math, the richest of Puri, as receiver of the temple properties and supervisor of the rituals and services.

At one time there were as many as 752 Maths in Puri town. They represented various sects such a Vaishnavism (Sri Sampradaya or Ramanuja, Ramanandi, Kabir Panthi, Khaki, Mulak Dasi, Vallabhachari, Madhwachari, Nimarka, Gaudiya, Radha Vallabhui, Gadwas Madhawa, etc.), Saivism (Dandi, Dasnami, Avaduta, Naga), Sakta (Dakhina, Vani, etc.) and miscellaneous sects of Nanak, Satanami and Sunyavadi types. This shows that some Maths follow monism, some dualism, and others special forms of dualism. In philosophy, and ideology, in the manner of worship and in their relationship with the temple of Lord Jagannath the Maths present a diversity but one thing which is common to all is their peaceful coexistence in Puri town and their ritual dedication and sub-ordination to the Jagannath Cult. Essentially the monasteries in their interrelatedness are integrated to the core of the sacred complex as one of its important aspects.

The heads of these monasteries, who are called by various titles such as Mahanta, Adhikari, Saraswati, Mahanta Maharaj, etc., are not only spiritual guides of the public but also scriptural advisors to the Gajapati Kings of Orissa and other administrative staff of the temple. Having vast landed properties in their possession some Maths are noted for their wealth. Although the latter wield more economic power and influence than other monasteries of moderate or low means, the public regard all of them as equal in the ritual sphere. Most of the Maths of Vaishnava sect possess large landed estates (Amrut Manohi) which were donated by their followers with the intention that the proceeds thereof should be spent in offering food (Bhog) to Lord Jagannath and the consecrated food (Mahaprasad) thus obtained should be distributed among the pilgrims, beggars, and ascetics. In brief the monastic houses act as strong connecting links between the public and the temple of Lord Jagannath, and perpetuate the sacred tradition of the pilgrim centre.

The Cultural Centres of Puri
(Parab Jatras, Akhada and Jegaghars, Sahi Jatra)

Wards and Sahis

Puri town has many *Sahis* (streets), some of which are larger and older and others are of later developments as extensions of original ones. The old records maintained by the temple scribe show that there were seven main sahis. They are Bali sahi, Dolamandap sahi, Goudabada sahi, Harachandi sahi, Kundeibenta Sahi, Markendeswar sahi and Matimandapa sahi. The other sahis and localities are Baddei sahi, Balagandi sahi, Baseli sahi, Chadaganga sahi, Dandinals sahi, Daita Sahi, Dhanakathi sahi, Ganamala sahi, Gudia sahi, Gurruntee sahi, Karagouri sahi, Kalikadebi sahi, Karati sahi, Kapal mochana, Khatua sahi, Khuntia sahi, Kumuti sahi, Manikarnika sahi, Mausima, Pathuria sahi, Patna Jenapur, Patna

Jagannathpur, Patna Balabhadra Ballava, Patna Matipada, Patna balisahi, Patna Parrhee sahi, Patna Kumbharpada, Patna Tikarpada and Talichha sahi.

As pointed out above the sahis which are situated close to the Jagannath temple are inhabited by the sebakas of the temple and there are also minor temples, monastic houses, lodging houses, sacred trees and tanks, gymnastic centres or youth organizations called *Jagaghar* and *Akhada* scattered in different *sahis* throughout the town.

Sahi Organization

Each of the main seven *sahis* has four headmen designated as Sahi Naik. They have assistants of barber caste who are called *Bhandari*. Among the young and adult men of the each sahi 16 able bodied adult men are chosen as *Bhendias* (*bhendia* means a strong and stout young men). The *Bhendias* work as wrestling instructors of *Jagaghars*, the club houses located in the sahis where the young and adult men practise gymanstic performances. Several *jagaghars* combine and function under the control of a bigger organization called *Akhada*.

The members of a *Jagaghar* are called *Sanga* (comrades). One who wants to be a *sanga* of a *jagaghar* should perform a ritual in which vermillion is anointed to the Mahabir, the presiding deity of the jagaghar and provide feast to the members. The nonmembers can learn gymnastic fits at the *jagaghar*, but they cannot be taken as members of it.

The *Naiks* of a *sahi* play an important role in organizing dance, drama and cultural performances related to various themes of sacred scriptures. Just as the Sebakas of the Jagannath temple have specific duties to perform as assigned by the Gajapati Raja of Puri and codified in the service record (*Karmani*) the Naiks of Sahis were also similarly assigned certain responsibilities which were also specified in the record of services. The nature of works which are entrusted to the Naiks is reproduced below from the service record.

"Four *sebaka* brahmins will remain in charge of *Naiks* in each sahi. They will be the head of all sebakas, royats, shop keepers and others of the sahi. All people of the sahi should cooperate with the Naiks so that they can function most effectively. Each household of sebaka community will pay a fee to the Naiks. Similarly the royats will also pay tax (Karachali) to them. A fee of one anna per rupee will be levied on each sale transaction of homestead land, orchard, etc. and given to the *Naiks*. They will set up a centre for cultural performance (*Akhada*) and enrol the Brahmin children in the centre and engage dance and drama experts to teach music and dance to these children. The expert drummers (*Madeli*) may also be appointed to teach them how to play on drums and help them to perform drama on themes selected from sacred scriptures and also narrations (Bachanika) on those subjects. The instructors giving training on these cultural performances will be given new cloths every month"

"The Naiks will see that fiestas and festivals such as birth ceremony of Krishna (Krishna janma) starting from the birth upto killing Kansa (Kansa Badha) and birth of Rama (Rama janma) are performed in the Sahis. In the case of Rama Janma all festivals starting from his birth to the killing of Ravana and thereafter to coronation ceremony will have to be performed. Similarly festivals connected with Baban Janma, Bali Raja and Sutanata during Devi parab will be performed. The divine play which is an aesthetic performance between Krishna and Radha and Gopies popularly known as *Rasalila* of the types such as Brindaban bihar, Basanta Rasa, Sarad Rasa etc., should be performed. During these festivals fire works, lighting of torches and candles beating of drums, singing of songs, decorations in multicoloured cloths of the pandals and places of worship will have to be arranged. When the Gajapati Raja is present in the palace at Bali Sahi in Puri the *Naiks* will show all these cultural performances to the Raja at the palace and thereafter proceed to the temple where they will repeat the same performances. As per the orders of the Raja the concerned parties will be given saris. The required quantity of oil used for lighting purposes will be supplied to them".

"On the Siva Ratri the *Naiks* will arrange performances of the type called *Ananda Nata* at the temple of Astasambhu. They will also provide labourers (*Bethia*) as recruited from different sahis to draw the cars up to the temple. Whatever contributions and incomes are received from festivals will be given to the *Naiks* for their personal use. If there will be shortage of funds which are required for the performances of such fiestas and festivals the *Naiks* will meet that amount from their pocket".

It is necessary to give a detailed account of organizations of some important sahis. The description is started with Markendaswar sahi.

Markendaswar Sahi

The first king of Ananta Verma Chodaganga Dev of Ganga dynasty built the temple of Sri Markedaswar Dev and adjoining minor temples during the middle part of the 11th century and established a settlement there. In this settlement he got the Devadasis settled and as population increased subsidiary hamlets sprang up near the main settlement. The most important hamlets which were later on called as Sahis are Chudanga Sahi, Hadagadia sahi, Banambar sahi, Ratha sahi, Bimanbadu sahi and Baseli sahi.

In the Markendaswar sahi and its subsidiary sahis now live such categories of sebakas as *Biman Badu, Paniapata, Kottasuaansia, Dalabehera, Supakar, Pandasamanta, Jatri Panda* (Jatri) and among others who live there such castes as *Khandayat, Teli, Mahanty, Tanti* and *Gudia* are important. The sebakas of *Kottasuansia, Paniapata* and *Dalabehera* belong to *Khandayat* caste, Ballava seba to *Gudia* group, and *Chakradihudi* and *Khalilagi* sebas to Gola caste.

In Markendaswar sahi there is a *Akhada* called Bhagabati Kotha Akhada under which seven *Jagaghars* are present. They are 1. Rahasa Mahanty, 2. Bhatta jaga, 3. Satabakhara, 4. Badapokhari, 5. Duari jaga, 6. Panda jaga and 7. Bada Mahapatra jaga. Each *jagaghar* is called panchayat having a president and other office bearers. A short description of Duari jaga is given below.

Duari Jaga

Raja Chodaganga Dev conferred *'Duari'* title on leading agriculturists and employed them in the temple. The service of a *Duari* is of the nature of checking food stuffs required for preparing bhog and watching at the door of the kitchen and outside it also. He was entitled to hold cane while on duty. Among them there was an important man named Basu Duari who was most favourite of the Raja of Puri. He was a great Tantrik like the then Raja of Puri and therefore in recognization of his *tantrik* qualities a *jagaghar* named as *Duari* was established in Markendaswar sahi. The *Duari jagaghar* or panchayat comprises a President, a vice-president, a Secretary and an Assistant Secretary, a Treasurer and 10 executive members. In all there are 100 members of the Panchayat varying in age within 25-60 years of age-group. The office bearers continue in their respective positions so long as everything goes well in the panchayat. However the office bearers are changed every three years. All members of the panchayat sit at the *jagaghar* and select the office bearers. Unarfimity rather than majority vote governs the selection of office bearers. One who becomes a member of the panchayat need not pay any fee. He has only to spend something for anointing the goddess of the panchayat with vermilion.

The *Duari jaga* owns a building and land of Ac. 1.500 adjoining it. The presiding deity Mahabir is the owner of the homestead land and other lands of *jagaghar*. It has also a beautiful garden called *Ramitota* which belongs to the goddess Ramchandi attached to the *jagaghar*. The temple of Ramachandi which is 15ft. in height with a platform of 30ft. × 40 ft. which is attached to it and a pond are located in the garden. A priest is appointed by the Sangas of *jagaghar* to worship the goddess.

Dasara is observed at Ramchandi and a feast is prepared on the last Tuesday of the month of *Chaitra*. All the *Sangas* perform these festivals together. A sum of Rs. 200/-is spent on the feast. Public contribution is also used in the performance of festivals and preparation of feast.

The *jagaghar* has an annual income of Rs. 1400/- from various sources such as sale proceeds of cashew nut, coconut, polanga (a kind of seed yielding oil), fruits and fuel, and from fish reared in the tank and miscellaneous sources. Besides these sources they all collect in kind and cash from the passers-by who pass through the road by the side of which the *jagaghar* is located. The people carrying cartloads of fuelwood along that road give some fuelwood to the *jagaghar.* Similarly the brick makers who pass by that road donate some bricks and those with thatching straw put some bundles of straw while passing through the road. Several cases are referred to *jagaghar* for arbitration, and the persons involved in such cases have to pay fees which are deposited in the fund of *jagaghar* and the party considered guilty is generally fined by the members of *jagaghar*. These fines are collected then and there and deposited in the funds of *jagaghar*.

There are also several other sources from which the jagaghar earns some income. For example, when the tank called *Markeanda* located in the sahi is renovated by a contractor some amount is collected from him. The major portion of this amount is credited to the panchayat's fund and some amount is distributed among its members. Close to the tank live many fishermen of *Gokha* caste. When they are engaged to catch fish in the Markanda tank they give one fourth of the catch to the *jagaghar*.

The cases in which there is nothing confidential are adjudicated in the place where Mahabir is installed and those which are of confidential nature are tried in the temple of goddess Ramchandi.

The *Jagaghar* has to perform certain rituals connected with the temple of Sri Jagannath. It has to offer *Panti bhog* to Sri Sudarsan on the day of *Gamha Purnima* and on *Chakrabula Ekadasi* to Sri Krishna on the *Kaliadalana Ekadasi* to Badi Nrusingh, on the 9th day of Swing festival, and to goddess Lakshmi on the day of Rusi Panchami. According to the sacred scriptures Markanda Rusi is the manager of the store of the goddess Lakshmi. He renders accounts of the store to the goddesss on the Rusi Panchami day, Mung, fried rice, cucumber, green coconut, etc, are offered to the deities in the panti bhog and a sum of Rs. 100/-is spent on this account.

As pointed out above the jagaghar has a good mango grove and the mangoes from this garden are offered to the deities and consumed by the members of the panchayat. Some times some mangoes are also distributed among the people of the sahi.

The members observe the birthday of Sri Mahabir on *Pana Sankranti* and spend about Rs. 100/-on this occasion. Similarly they also observe Asokastami for which the members meet all the expenses out of their own pocket.

The *jagaghar* takes up new constructions and undertake repairing of the existing buildings and temples, renovates the tanks and maintains the garden properly. The buildings under its procession are all electrified for which a sum of Rs. 200/-is paid and the rent for the land amounting Rs. 10/-is paid to the Government.

The *jagaghar* has a spacious building used for gymnasium. The male members who are agnates of the members of the panchayat are allowed to attend physical training at this place. There is sufficient room for 10 people to practise physical exercise daily. Those who take part in gymnastic exercise also learn the skills of playing on drums particularly the type known as *Pakhaja* which is very popular among the sebakas.

There are two instructors for imparting physical training, one music teacher and an instrumentalist teaching the trainees the art of singing and playing on musical instruments and drums. All these instructors belong to Markendaswar sahi. The instructors hold their classes at the *jagaghar* two hours in the morning and two hours in the afternoon. The Government of Orissa had given a grant of Rs. 2000/- to the panchayat towards the expenses of musical instruments.

In the Markendaswar sahi the following items of cultural shows are performed:

1. *Putanabadha* (A demon names Putana who was trying to feed poison to Sri Krishna was killed by him).

2. *Jamuna Gadhua* (bathing in the river Jamuna). This is a scene of Gopis taking bath in the Jamuna river).

3. *Sri Krishna janma* (birth of Sri Krishna).

In the fiestas performed in the Sahi (Sahi jata) the following categories of actors take part most prominently.

1. *Sandhiasi* : The young boys dressed in half pants (*Janghia*), white caps and holding sword show various accrobatic and gymnastic performances.

2. *Naga* : A man is dressed like a *Paik*. The things which make up the dress of a Paik are knife held in hand, shield (*Dhala*) tied to the arm, sword (*talabar*) held in hand, battle axe (*Katuri*), arm band (*Bahuti*), bells (*Ghanti*), tied to thigh and waist, tiger's skin (*Baghachhala*), tiger' nail (*Bagha nakha*), gun (*Bandhuka*), head gear (*Handia*).

3. *Meda* : *Meda* is a wooden structure decorated beautifully with coloured clothes and other materials and having seats for the deities to be installed and for men to sit and dance, etc. The meda is named after the deity which is being installed in it or after the occasion on which it is prepared. Thus there are Durga meda (meda for Siva and Durga), Kalika meda (meda for goddess Kali), Nrusingh meda (meda for Sri Nrusingh).

4. *Sattara* : A *Sattara* does not wear any head gear. He uses sticks to produce rhythm while singing. He sings only devotional songs.

Holding a banner (*nisana*) of red cloth which is called Mahibir Nisana a man sits on an elephant and leads the procession comprising the above mentioned actors in the following order-*Sandhiasi, Meda, Palabala,* (recitors of sacred texts), *Kela* and *Keluni* (a man taking the place of Kela caste-an untouchable and his wife) Sattara and Naga. As the procession proceeds the people at interval go on shouting the following couplet.

Mar Pathar Toda Darwaja Kileki Dewal
(Throw stone, break open door, pull down wall)
Raban, sala Gharme Chhupe Dikho Inka Hal
(Wife's brother Ravana hides himself in the house and see his plight)

The procession starts from the *jagaghar.* All people accompanying the procession have *darsan* of *Patitapaban* and go out of the temple through the southern gate. They proceed along the Lokanath road and come to the *Bada Akhada jagaghar* where they take rest and undress themselves. From there they come to the place where Sri Sanketaswar temple is located. It is located at a *ghat* and from this ghat they sail by boat to the mouth of Harachandi. In the boat the boys will be dancing and some people will be grinding *bhanga* an intoxicant mixed in water to drink. It is most popular drink among the sebakas. From the mouth of Harachandi they proceed to a place called Narasingh Patna. It is at this place that the garland of order of Sri Jagannath is offered to the goddess Harachandi. The *Mahaprasad* carried with them is also offered to the goddess. A goat is sacrificed and offered to the goddess. Thereafter they return to Narasingh Patna belonging to the Pandit math. They stay there for two days and spend time in eating and drinking. Varieties of food, fish and mutton are cooked and eaten and the time is spent in great merriment. The party returns to Puri after two days.

As regards other *Jagaghar* every one has a history of origin and used to perform festivals with equal elaborations as is done by the *Duari jagaghar.* But for the last two decades or so some of them have altogether stopped performing such fiestas. The *Jagaghars* such as *Panda jega* and *Satabakara* have been performing Ashokastami and *Bhatta jega* continues the festival or Nrusingh chaturdasi.

In other sahis there are similar Akhadas and Jagaghars. They have each a history of origin, organizational arrangements, specific fiestas and festivals to perform and ritual associations with the temple. However, under the influence of modern times the festivities and other functions such as physical training and musical performances show a great deal of attenuation in most cases.

The different sahis are not separate entities. They are connected with one another in various ways. One of the media through which they are more intimately associated with one another is the festive ceremonies which are performed in different sahis. These are called *Sahijatra* (festivals of sahis). For a better understanding of the inter relationship between the sahis it is necessary to give an account of the *sahijatra*.

The *sahijatra* starts from the 9th days of the bright half of the month of *chaitra*. The seven principal sahis of Puri perform these festivals in cooperation with one another. On the 9th day of the bright half of the month of *Chaitra* a festive procession comprising Rama, Lakshman, Bharat, Satrughna and Sita with Rusyasrunga starts from the *Akhada* of Kalikadebi sahi. It is on this day that the birth ceremony of Rama is observed in the temple. The party proceeds to the temple and after having *darshan* of Sri Jagannath who is adorned with the dress of Rama and receiving the garland of order (Agnya Mala) from Sri Jagannath leaves the temple and visits different maths and collects some contribution from each of them and then visits some important houses and also collects some contribution from them and thereafter returns to their sahi.

On the 10th day another festive party called *Nakakana* (nose and ear) starts from Harachandi sahi. The people comprising the party represent the demons. They dress themselves like demons and start from the *Akhada* of Harachandi sahi. Dancing and singing in accompaniment of music they enter the Bali sahi and from there they proceed to the temple and then finally reach Jagannath Ballava Math. At this math they undress themselves and there that day's part of the festival is finished.

On the 11th day the epic hero Parsuram starts his journey from the Akhada of Harachandi Sahi. No other castes except the sebakas can play the part of Parsuram and the privilege of being dressed like Parsuram is confined to three or four families of Harachandi Sahi and it is these families which act as Parsuram on a hereditary basis. However a change has come about in this regard. In the last 8 to 10 years other people having good physique are acting as Parsuram.

The Parsuram visits the houses of noted families and recites his valor and deeds and collects contributions from them. He does this for two days and on the last day after having darsan of Sri Jagannath goes to Jagannath Ballava Math where he is killed. These are all theatrical actions, nothing real. For this purpose three members of the *Akhada* of Markandaswar Sahi dressed as Rama, Lakshman and Sita proceed from their *sahi* to Jagannath Ballava Math through the temple of Sri Jagannath and fight with Parsuram and kill him. It is known that the acting of Parsuram was not originally of the Harachandi sahi. But three decades back the Matimandap sahi had transferred this festival on sale from their *Akhada* to that of Harachandi sahi.

The Sasan Villages, Muktimandapa and Pandits

Of all the infrastructure set up by the Gajapati Rajas for the perpetuation of the Sacred Complex the

Brahminical tradition was the most fundamental. The institutional form of this tradition is the Brahmin settlements called Sasan which they established within 10 miles of the sacred centre of Purusottam and had them associated with the temple through the Muktimandapa, the seat of the pandits representing these settlements for the perpetuation of the traditions of the Sacred Complex and the Jagannath temple.

The Gajapati Rajas have in all established 16 Sasans and 32 Karabadas (Sub-settlements) within a radius of 10 miles from Puri. The Hindu Kings brought the Brahmins to Orissa from Western and Northern India and granted them villages which they hold at a tanki rent (quit-rent) or free of rent on Sanads (deeds by which grants of lands and villages were made by the rulers) describing the terms and conditions of the grant. They also granted the Brahmins lands upon which to live and build temples and have tanks dug at which they could perform their daily rituals and seasonal festivals.

The Sasani Brahmins are exclusively devoted to the study of Vedas, and Dharma granthas, and to discussions and contemplation on topics concerning Sanskritic Hinduism and the Hindu way of life. They were equally competent and expert in military techniques and warfare. The most learned and orthodox Brahmins of the Sasan villages worked in Muktimandapa as Councilors to the Gajapati Rajas and the Jagannath temple on matters of spiritual and scriptural importance such as the reading of omens, the best modes of averting the bad effects of some of them, and on other business of consequence deemed necessary for the management of the affairs of the temples.

The best of all Brahmins of the Sasan villages who had acquired skill and competence in military techniques and sound knowledge on scriptural literature was appointed as the Prime Minister of the Gajapati Rajas. He led the Gajapatis to the battle field and fought against the enemy and protected the kingdom against aggression. On the whole the guardianship and leadership of the Brahmin pandits in maintaining the Sanskritic traditions in perpetuity and in guarding against any deviation of the prescribed rites and duties performed in religious institutions by the ritual functionaries is most important.

The Brahmin pandits of Muktimandapa are consulted by the temple authorities about social usages and ritual matters pertaining to the temple. We state below four such questions which the temple manager placed before the Pandits and the decisions, which they gave on these issues.

The Minor Rajas of Feudatory States

Subordinate to the Gajapati Rajas are many minor Rajas of Feudatory States who are the guardians of the temples, Maths, Sasan villages located in their respective kingdoms. These religious and cultural institutions which are smaller in dimension are an integral part of the larger Sacred Complex of Puri. The Minor Rajas are connected with the Gajapati Rajas and the Jagannath Temple of Puri by a network of social, cultural and religious relationships and it is through these relationships that the Sacred Complex is maintained and perpetuated throughout Orissa. A sketch of the minor Rajas vis-à-vis the Gajapati Raja and the Sacred Complex is given below.

Raja Purusottam Deb (1465-1495) granted estates to the minor Rajas who paid tribute to him as a mark of subordination to him, and came to be known as Tributary Chiefs-Karada Raja. These minor Rajas served the Raja of Puri in various capacities as the Sebaks do to him. When the Raja comes out of his palace on a visit either to the temple or any other palace the minor Rajas are expected to accompany him and perform their respective duties as acts of respect. These duties are granted as marks of favour by the Raja of Puri, he being the paramount Raja of Orissa (Gajapati). A ceremony is observed in the Raja's court while bestowing such favours. This ceremony of bestowal is called *Sadi-Bandha*. The Sadi is a valuable piece of cloth, which is tied to the head of the person who is favoured to do a particular duty in honour of the Raja of Puri. The Sadi-Bandha is typical of conferring any favour, title, service or estate on any person. No Sebak of the temple is allowed to perform his rituals in the temples unless he undergoes the ceremony of Sadi-Bandha. Similarly no Mahanta of a monastery is recognized as such unless he undergoes the rituals of Sadi-Bandha. On this occasion the incumbent pays a fee called *Nazar* to the Raja who then orders the sacred cloth to be tied to his head and awards formal sanction to serve in the temple in the case of the Sebak or to act as a Mahanta of a Math. People of various categories seek various types of privileges of the Raja and the Raja confers upon them such privilege to perform by means of Sadi-Bandha which is nothing but a formal way of giving royal sanction and approval to the incumbents to enjoy such privileges.

How the noble man on whom was bestowed the honour of bearing the knife and dagger had his sight of Lord Jagannath is as follows.

Benudar Mangaraja of Badamba came on his own palanquin with his people to the temple for darsan of Lord Jagannath. He came at the time of the evening meal (Sandhya Dhupa). Candles were lighted in the temple enabling him to have a clear sight of the deity. He offered gifts (Pindika) and three pieces of a kind of cloth called Kala Mahuda. He circumambulated the temple and had a view of the minor deities and then left the temple.

Thus the minor Rajas of different feudatory States were offered Sadi-Bandha to do several kinds of duties in honour of the Raja of Puri.

A list of bestowals and services offered by the minor Rajas as obtained from the temple scribe is given below:

Name of the State	*Nature of duties entrusted to perform*
Tigiria	Parichha (to hold the golden cane)
Mayurbhanja	--do--
Talcher	To hold sword (Khanda)
Ranpur	To hold dagger and sword (Chhuri-Khanda)
Bamanda	To hold betel leaf receptacle (pana bata)
Nayagarh	To hold spittoon (Pikadani)

6

Definition and Typology of Sacred Centres in Terms of Sacred Geography and Culture Pattern

It is observed that the shrines and other symbols of worship such a tanks, trees, etc., related to certain sectarian and ritualistic considerations need to be classified for differentiating one from the other. Specific terms need to be used for such differtiations. In this connection what Vidyarthy has said in his book. The Sacred Complex in Hindu Gaya is reproduced below:

(A) Sacred Geography and Locational Significance*

If I look at these shrines and other symbols of worship closely, I note a certain locational significance which also can be related to certain sectarian and ritualistic considerations. I note the need for formulating terms like "sacred centre", "sacred cluster", "sacred segment", "sacred zone" and "sacred ground" to indicate, firstly, the location of one shrine in relation to another, and secondly, to help me in the precise analysis of some of the complexities of the sacredness of Gaya.

In the course of such a geographical survey of the various shrines and other symbols of worship, I feel the need of calling the smallest unit of worship, represented by an image, river, tank, or tree, the sacred centre. A sacred centre represents a single spot where a sacred performance takes place. Such a sacred centre may be variously located. It may be isolated, as I observe is the case in a number of Shiva temples (Shivalaya), the houses of epic deities (thakurbadi), or other types of sacred centres scattered in the city. Then, a sacred centre may be in a cluster of many other sacred centres in its adjacent neighbourhood. For example, I discover Manglagauri is in a cluster of sacred centres devoted to Shiva, Krishna, and Vishnu; Ramshila is in a cluster of sacred centres dedicated to Shiva, Ram, and Yama; and Pretashila combines in itself several centres-Pretashila, Pretabhavani, and Vishnu. Similarly, In Old Gaya several clusters of sacred centre surrounding such dominant sacred centres as Vishnupada, the Phalgu, the Surya temple, Gayeshvari, and Gaya Sir may be distinguished. In the northern margin of Old Gaya there are the two sacred clusters of Pitamheshvar and Sitla. To denote such a combination of sacred centres around a dominant sacred centre, the term "sacred cluster" has been used. Usually such sacred clusters are under a single set of priests. They also might be characterized by a single set of sectarian deities. There are notable exceptions, however, to this rule. At Manglagauri, we notice sacred centres devoted to Vishnu and Shiva; at Ramshila, we find non-Brahmanical deities of ghosts in addition to Shaiva and Vaishnava deities. In a cluster of sacred centres, however, the form of worship is usually modified according to the dominant sacred centre. For example, in the Manglagauri and Bageshvari clusters, where the goddess mother forms the dominant sacred centre, the rites of animal sacrifice continue in spite of the fact that the sacred centres dedicated to Shiva and Vishnu happen to be there in close proximity. Similarly, the goddesses Sitla and Gayeshvari, located in the neighbourhood of the vegetarian dominant sacred centres Pitamaheshvar and Vishnupada, respectively, are never worshipped with any type of animal sacrifice.

On another locational and organizational level, two or more clusters forming a continuous segment may be termed a "sacred segment". At this level, the Vishnupada-Phalgu-Surya Mandir Gayeshvari-Gaya Sir group would form one sacred segment; Pitamaheshvar-Uttarmanas-Sitla would form another; Mangalagouri-Akshayavat would form a third; and far to the north, Bageshvari-Ramshila would be still a fourth sacred segment. On the segmental level, the combination and compromise of different types of symbolic representation, the various types of sectarian deities, and several orders of priesthood find full expression. Let me illustrate this point by referring to the Vishnupada-Phalgu-Surya Mandir-Gayaeshvari-Gaya Sir segment, which is the most celebrated and typically elaborated segment under our study.

In this segment all types of symbols or emblems of divinities and deities are presented. There are magnificent images of the sun god, various manifestations of Vishnu, as well as mystical idols represented by the Shiva shrine (Shivalaya) and the Vishnu pada. The Phalgu is the celebrated river and the Surya Kund is the important tank for the worship of the sun. There are two extremely large pipal trees in this sacred segment that receive occasional worship from the worshippers and sacrificers. In addition to all these sacred centres, there are almost countless deities represented by stones, images, engravings, and paintings, which are enshrined here and there on the wall shelves, under the trees, or near the larger temples. All of these add up to make the sacred segment the crowded city of deities.

Considered from the viewpoint of representation of the sectarian deities, all the five principal sects of the Hindus-Vishnava, Shaiva, Shakta, Saura, Ganpatyas-are represented. Though the segment is particularly sacred for the cult of Vishnu, the other sectarian deities are not neglected. The sacred centres devoted to the remaining sects are located in close proximity to the Vishnu sacred centres and are worshipped by the Hindus without much sectarian discrimination. The temple of the sun, in front of which is a tank called Surya Kund (sun tank), especially attracts a large crowd of devotees on the occasion of the Chhatha Vrata (Sun vow). The Gayeshvari is also an important sacred centre devoted to the goddess of power (Shakti), but as it is officiated by Dasnami priests and falls in the segment of Vaishnava dominance, there is no animal sacrifice. The Shiva sacred centre and the Ganesh sacred centre, which are each represented in this segment by one temple, are not so celebrated but receive offerings from the worshippers.

The coming together of priestly orders for maintaining and receiving gifts at different sacred centres of this segment is another interesting feature. The Gayawal priests are the custodians of the Vishnupada sacred centre, several families of the Sakadvip Brahman are the officiating priests of the sun temple, while mahants of the three orders of the Dasnami Sannyasi-Giri, Puri and Bharati (Buchanan1811-12: 111; Ghurye 1953: 924) who reside there in a matha share the gifts offered at the Gayeshvari sacred centre. All of these are priests belonging to the Brahman Varna but of different sectarian denominations. Two other sacred clusters, however, are officiated by the non-Brahman priesthood, about which mention will be made at the appropriate places.

Considered from the ritualistic point of view, the major sacred centres of this sacred segment are visited by the devotees from different motives. In the case of the

Vishnupada temple when 200 worshippers were interviewed on three specific days, thirty-five per cent made vague replies which, in essence, signified their intentions to worship for general reasons of health and prosperity. Forty per cent of the worshippers were more or less specific about their intentions-they came either to make offerings after the fulfillment of some vows or to made fresh vows. Their visits were related to the resolution of certain problems that confronted them or their families. Some of the specific problems were to secure jobs, to win suits, to pass in the school or college examinations, to succeed in business or in other new under replied that they wanted to earn merit for happiness in the next life, while two per cent of them were there to celebrate some initiation rites.

Though any sacred centre, or the combination of two or three, may be visited by worshippers with the above-mentioned or other purposes, sacred centres of this segment, as in the case of other sacred centres of other segment have become especially efficacious for the fulfillment of certain specific desires. For example, the Vishnupada and the Phalgu are especially celebrated for the shraddha sacrifice, while the Gayeshvari is particularly efficacious for securing a suitable husband or for childbirth. Visits to the sun temple and baths in the sun tank are especially undertaken to get rid of sickness like leprosy and other serious skin diseases.

The other sacred segments of Gaya-the Manglagauri-Akshayavat, the Pitamaheshvar-Uttarmanas-Sitla, and the Bageshvari Ramshila-bring out, more or less, the same characteristics as described for the Vishnupada-Phalgu-Surya Mandir-Gayeshvari sacred segment. But a sacred segment need not be considered as a complete organization. Segments are related to each other in the sense that a worshipper or sacrificer goes from one segment to another to make offerings to the deities. From the locational point of view, again, the sacred segments-Vishnupada-Phalgu Surya Mandir-Gayeshvari-Gaya Sir, the Manglagauri-Akshayavat, and the Pitamasheshvar-Uttarmanas Sital-can be categorized together to make one sacred zone so as to contrast it with the heterogeneous zone of secular Gaya. In the sacred zone, then, there are three sacred segments, which are more or less connected through the residence of priests and other sacred specialists. It is a zone of specialization for sacred activities and ritual performances. To summarize, then, in Gaya, I have been able to define a sacred zone of Old Gaya, one sacred segment of Ramshila-Bagheshvari, one sacred cluster of Pretashila, and several-isolated sacred centres, all of which fall within the sacred ground of Gaya.

(B) Cultural Pattern

The concept of pattern has been used in several rather different ways by anthropologists. Configurationalists used the term to refer to the constellations of formal features (or "styles") which characterize particular cultures. This Benedict, in Patterns of Culture (1934) classifies different cultures according to their dominant orientation (Dionysian, Apollonian etc.). The term may also be used to refer to culturally standardized behaviour patterns such as rituals, ceremonies, or simply customary or typical sequences of activity. Yet another use of the term is in Parson's (1963) concept of pattern variables or sets of alternative orientations towards social action. (Extract from Mc. Millan dictionary of Anthropology Page. 63)

The definition of Cultural Trait and Trait Complex is reproduced from the book Cultural Anthropology by N. K. Bose and Culture Pattern from the book Anthropology by A.L. Kroeber.

The Structure of a Cultural Trait*

Having cleared out mind regarding the general nature of culture as a whole, we shall proceed to define in the present chapter, a number of technical terms in use among anthropologists. We shall also see how these analytical concepts help to elucidate the problems of cultural history.

Cultural Trait-If we travel over a country like India and observe the habits and customs of its different provinces, an interesting things is soon brought to our notice. In Bengal the chief foodstuff consists of rice, which is prepared for food by simply boiling it in water. The indigenous dress of the country consists of an unseen piece of cloth and another similar piece to cover the upper part of the body. The head is bare, while the feet are shod in slippers, which only cover the forepart and leave the back of the foot bare. The cottages of Bengal are thatched with straw except in the bordering districts near Bihar, where semi-cylinderical tiles are also sometimes used for the same purpose. The Bengalis are divided into castes as in other provinces of India; but observing more closely, we find that the relation between different castes is not the same as in other provinces. The Vaishnava and Sakta religious sects prevail in this part of the country, while a number of magical rites are also in vogue among the inhabitants.

In the Punjab, on the other hand, wheat or millets may be said to form the principal food-stuff. Unlike rice, it is ground into flour and prepared in the form of thin cakes of bread. The fat in food is derived from cow's milk, while in Bengal it is also largely supplied by vegetable seeds like mustard. The dress of men and women in the Punjab consists of sewn trousers and upper garments. The head is turbaned, while the shoe covers the feet completely, both before and behind. No thatched houses are noticeable, all of them being tiled as in Bihar. The order of castes is different from that of Bengal. The prevailing religious sects consist of Sikhism and the Saiva form of Hinduism.

Instances of difference between the numerous provinces of India could easily be multiplied; but from what has been said, it will be quite clear that although the culture of different parts of India consists of material traits, social systems etc., yet the units forming each of them are entirely different in the case of each province. Each of these distinguishing units is termed a Trait in Anthropology.

The study of cultural traits gives us a convenient means of judging the influence of one culture over another, and of finding the path of diffusion of a particular trait. It is therefore necessary to enter into some details regarding the internal structure of a cultural trait.

Rice-It has already been said that rice forms one for the distinguishing traits of the material culture of Bengal. Let us observe for the moment what other cultural features have gathered round the principal foodstuff of the province.

The paddy fields of Bengal are ploughed with the aid of bullocks. They are harnessed to a yoke which has pegs inserted towards the middle in such a way as to prevent the animals from coming too close to each other when taking a corner. This type of yoke differs from that associated with bullock-carts in Bengal, the pegs of which are inserted near the outer extremities instead.

The grains of paddy are sown thickly in the field, whence they are transplanted to bigger fields after germination. The corn is cut with a sickle and threshed in the following manner. When brought freshly from the field, the sheaves of corn are beaten upon a threshing board. After as much grain as possible has been separated in this way, they are spread upon the ground and bullocks driven round and round over them. A man, now and then, rakes up the sheaves lying below. When the threshing operation is over, the grains of paddy are either boiled or steeped in water for husking. Husking is performed by means of an apparatus called the *Dhenki*. It consists of a huge wooden lever attached to a stand near one of its ends. A short pestle is fixed perpendicularly at the end of the longer section of the beam. The lever is raised by one or two persons stepping upon the shorter section of the beam. By stepping off, the pestle is made to drop into a hole in the ground, which is lined with stone, in which the grains are put in for husking.

Rice is boiled for food in a large quantity of water of which the surplus is thrown away. On festive occasions, rice may be ground into flour and either prepared in the form of thin sheets of bread or a variety of cakes called *Pitha*. Rice which is not boiled for husking is considered to be pure and may be used in religious ceremonies. Widows and orthodox Brahmins partake of this form of rice only. Powdered sun-dried rice is also made into emulsion with water for drawing artistic designs on the walls or floor of a house in religious celebrations.

There are again a number of caste-restrictions attaching to rice. A person belonging to an inferior caste may accept cooked rice from one belonging to a higher caste; and this is regarded as the chief test of caste-superiority. When a girl first enters her father-in-law's house after marriage, she is made to serve cooked rice to members of the caste, signifying her formal entry into its fold. The same procedure is adopted when an excommunicated person re-enters his caste after the purificatory ceremonies. When a person dies in a house or a child is born, the ceremonial impurity of the family is indicated by other people abstaining from eating rice in that house. Thus, rice plays an important part in social as well as ceremonial questions in Bengal.

But its use does not stop here. There are also a number of magical practices connected with rice. When an article is stolen from a house, an Ojha (a shaman) might be called in to detect the miscreant. He takes a quantity of rice, utters magical formulas over it and distributes a handful to each of the suspects. The latter are asked to chew the rice thoroughly and spit it out in the end. It is believed that the real culprit is sure to spit out a quantity of blood along with the rice.

Definition of Elements and Trait Complex

A large number of cultural items have thus gathered round the chief foodstuff of the province of Bengal. The consists of material traits like a distinctive type of yoke, the Dhenki and so on; ceremonial elements like the caste-rules of beliefs regarding the purity or otherwise of certain forms of rice; and finally a number of magical practices. Each of these isolable units is called an element in Anthropology, while in their entirety the elements are said to form a Trait or Trait-Complex.

The Continuity of Culture

The continuity of a specific culture depends upon the transmission of such material traits as rice in the above example. The children of one generation of the Bengalis learn about the use or rice from their fathers and they also imbibe the same beliefs and imitate the same processes of action, which characterised the rice-complex in the days of their fathers. In this manner, the beliefs, ideas and habits of a culture are handed on from generation to generation through the intermediary of concrete objects of some sort or other. It might be an article like rice, or it might be an institution with its economic assets and liabilities, which acts as the vehicle for transmission of culture through the ages.

In a similar manner when a culture is transmitted from one tribe to another, the main transmission takes place in relation to a number of material objects.

Variation of a Trait Complex

This leads us on to an important character of trait-complexes, namely, their variability in relation to time and space. It has already been said that the beliefs and opinions of men change according to their historical experiences. Each trait of culture accordingly has a different meaning in each successive age. In other words, the character of the trait is also modified in course of time.

Then again, the trait might vary owing to transference from one tribe to another. A foreign trait can only become part of the culture of another tribe after it has been recast in accordance with the prevailing patterns of that culture and has also gathered round it associational ties with established trait-complexes. The original divergence of a trait from its character in the parent culture arises in this way. But as time goes on, the points of different increase in number as the two cultures proceed along their own courses of historical change. Isolation from one another also helps to widen the gulf of difference.

Classification and Examples of Variable Traits

The actual variation in a trait-complex is brought about by one of the following processes; (1) the addition of new elements, (2) dropping of old ones or (3) their modification in accordance with changed public opinion or other patterns of culture. Among these, the second principle is of more than special importance. It has an intimate relation with the spatial distribution of a trait and will therefore be illustrated in the following chapter. We shall close the present chapter with examples of the other kinds of variation.

The Holi-festival of India originally formed a part of a certain non-vedic culture, regarding which we do not know very much. But it appears to have been performed with a human sacrifice, followed by that of a sheep on the following day. The sheep was committed to the flames along with the entrails of the human victim killed previously. When the festival was incorporated in Hinduism, the human sacrifice could no longer be permitted. So it was replaced by the burning of a human effigy or of a sheep or its effigy. In one case at least, no effigy is employed, but a man is compelled to jump through the flames of a bonfire. The change might be said to have been due either to changed public opinion or incorporation into a culture in which the ideas associated with the trait could no longer be tolerated.

But we meet with a better example of the latter in the Sun-cult of India. During the early centuries of the Christian era, the worship of the Sun god of Persia was introduced by certain Magi refugees into India. The Indians were used to the worship of the Vedic Sun god even before these people came; so that the new cult soon became associated with a number of Vedic elements. In this state it was introduced into Orissa sometime about the 10th century A.D.

The prevailing cult of Orissa was connected with a deity named Jagannath. The form of worship of this particular deity is as follows. He is treated as a person belonging to a very high rank. Food is offered to him several times in the day; and the chief festive occasion connected with the deity is the car festival. At Puri, where the temple of Jagannath is situated, sixteen small shrines dedicated to eight forms of Siva and their consorts are distributed over an area sacred to the deity. At Konark too when the Sun-god, introduced from Persia, came to have a temple built in his honour, the same number of shrines were erected over the area held sacred to him. The daily routine of worship followed that of Jagannath; while a car-festival was similarly instituted at that place. The Persian sun-cult thus gathered new elements in India, and was also recast into a definite pattern in one of its provinces. As a matter of fact, it would not have been possible to identify the Sun-god at Konark with the original Magi Sun-god, had it not been for literary references to the Magi priests and certain important features in the iconography of that deity.

A trait-complex gathers new element in course of time, such elements not forming an essential part of the trait. Technically, such variation is said to be due to secondary accumulation. An apt illustration comes from the Holy-festival, which we have already discussed in a different context. In the town of Lahore, one of the rites held in connection with the Holi is formed by a number of men masquerading through public streets in the guise of popular gods. In some parts of the Punjab again the festival is celebrated with wrestling tournaments. Then again, in Benares, it is customary to gamble on the night of the Holi; while in Bengal presents are sent to the houses of friends and relatives. They consist of a special preparation of peas and grams in molasses and of miniature temples made of sugar. The accretion of such elements naturally increases with time and isolation between countries observing the same trait.

The Infrequency of Inventions

Among the processes of modification which have been considered above, it should be noted that the addition of absolutely new elements is much less frequent than the other three processes of change. As a matter of fact, the elaboration of a trait into many varieties is caused not so much by the appearance of absolutely new ideas and forms, as by the addition of elements from other cultural traits of a like character. New ideas are very rare in cultural history; they are as infrequent as mutants are in biology. Newness generally comes from the rearrangement of parts, or by the reshaping of an acquired trait in accordance with a pattern which may itself be old. Newness through the addition of new elements is a rare phenomenon in history.

The history of culture can be compared to the flow of a broad river near its mouth; where new eddies are created not by the inflow of tributary streams, but by the interplay of the little currents which altogether made up the body of the river.

Summary-A trait is an isolable and distinguishing unit of a culture, which, is an intimate assemblage of certain actions, sentiments, attitudes and objects. Each of the isolable elements which enters into the composition of a trait is known as an element.

Traits are variable in character. They change through spatial distribution of a change in the mental outlook. Modification is brought about by the addition of new elements, dropping of old ones or recasting in accordance with changed public opinion or other patterns of culture.

Speaking in terms of Culture the following terms can serve as substitutes of the geographic terms used by Vidyarthy. The cultural terms are "Cultural Element", "Cultural Trait", "Cultural Trait Complex", "Cultural Pattern and Cultural Area".

The term Cultural Element and Cultural Trait can be used in place of Sacred Centre. Cultural Trait-Complex in place of Sacred Cluster, Cultural pattern-Patterns are those arrangements or systems of internal relationship which give to any culture its coherence or plan and keep it from being a mere accumulation of random bits. In place of Sacred Segment, Cultural Area in place of Sacred Zone and Sacred Ground

(C) Short Account of the Sacred Centres (Numbering 127) Showing their Locations in the Sketch of Sankha Kshetra

The holy trinity-Lord Balabhadra, Maa Subhadra and Lord Jagannath are installed on the Ratnasinhasan along with Surdarsan and some other minor deities. In the compound of Lord Jagannath temple there are many deities enshrined in their respective temples in the inner compound. Similarly there are some sacred centres located in the outer compound. The deities of the temple itself and those all around the temple including both the inner and outer compound made a sacred zone.

Like wise there are many deities installed either singly or in clusters in their respective shrines all over the Sankha Kshetra. They form another sacred zone. Central to these two zones is the Jagannath Temple including both the inner and outer compound.

The deities belonging to these two zones are distributed in different folds. There are seven folds each fold comprising the temples of the deities belonging to the above mentioned two zones. An account of these seven folds is given below or zones.

These folds correspond to sacred segment. Thus there are seven segments which cover all the sacred places. The discussions regarding the segments follow short account of each of the sacred centres located in the whole of Puri Pilgrim centre.

Sankha Kshetra includes the following shrines and temples, tanks, tree and some other sacred places. A list of these sacred places existing in the Geography of the Sankha Kshetra is given below:

Name of the Sacred Items

(1) Shrimandir

(2) Shri Khyatraswari (Bimala)

(3) Shri Mahalaxmi

(4) Uttar Durga

(5) Batamangala

(6) Garuda Sthamba

(7) Bhoga Mandap

(8) Kalpabata

(9) Rohini Kunda

(10) Bata Ganesh

(11) Uchista Ganapati

(12) Saraswati

(13) Nabagraha

(14) Konark Suryadeb

(15) Padapadma

(16) Jagyumbata

(17) Satyanarayan

(18) Sakhigopinath

(19) Jayabijaya

(20) Agnyeswara

(21) Indrani (Badreswari)

(22) Kshetrapala

(23) Swanabhairavi

(24) Mukteswar

(25) Ghorakali

(26) Bata Markendeswara

(27) Katyayani Budhima

(28) Gopeswarim

(29) Bedhakali

(30) Pataleswari

(31) Bhubaneswari

(32) Baikunthaswara

(33) Jagyeswari

(34) Aisanyaeswari

(35) Shitala

(36) Bhetamandapa

(37) Pakashala

(38) Dakhineswari

(39) Kundalaswara

(40) Gauranga

(41) Shriram

(42) Barabhai Hanuman

(43) Nirmalaya Hanuman

(44) Upaana Alakabatika

(45) Rameswar

(46) Chakranarayan

(47) Chaturdham

(48) Kanpata Hanuman

(49) Niladribihari

(50) Bayubyeswara

(51) Adagdha Sialilata

(52) Koili Baikuntha

(53) Tapaswsi Hanuman

(54) Subarna Kupa

(55) Ananda Bazar Kaiblya Pasara

(56) Deba Snanha Mandap

(57) Chahani Mandapa

(58) Baisi Pabachha

(59) Kashi Biswanath

(60) Phate Hanuman

(61) Patitapaban

(62) Singhadwar

(63) Meghanada Acheri

(64) Badachhata Matha

(65) Uttar (Hati) Dwar

(66) Paschima (Byaghra) Dwara

(67) Mangaleswari

(68) Durgamadhaba

(69) Dakhina (Aswa) Dwara

(70) Prahari Hanuman

(71) Chhauni Matha

(72) Aruna Stamba

(73) Jagannath Ballava

(74) Narendra Puskarani

(75) Bisweswari

(76) Dolabedi

(77) Makardhwaja Hanuman

(78) Alamba Devi

(79) Atharanala

(80) Bhargabi Nadi

(81) Saptamatruka

(82) Markanda (Tank)

(83) Markandeswara

(84) Bhagabati

(85) Banadurga

(86) Ghatamangala

(87) Chamundeswari

(88) Harachandi

(89) Panduashram

(90) Nikumbhila Bata

(91) Kandu Nrushinha

(92) Parvati Sagar

(93) Sri Lokanath

(94) Jambeswar

(95) Baseli

(96) Kappal Mochan

(97) Mani Karnika (Tank)

(98) Barahi Devi

(99) Shyamakali

(100) Shankaracharya Math

(101) Mukti Shala

(102) Sweta Ganga (Tank)

(103) Ugreswara Ashrama

(104) Dakhina Kali

(105) Siddha Bakula Matha

(106) Narayani

(107) Sodasaputri

(108) Marchika Devi

(109) Charchika Devi

(110) Ardhasosani Mausimaa

(111) Daria Hanuman

(112) Chakra Narayan

(113) Chakra Tirtha

(114) Sri Gundicha Mandir

(115) Adi Nrusinha Nath

(116) Nilakantheswar

(117) Indra Dumna (Tank)

(118) Siddha Hanuman

(119) Beleswar

(120) Mukteswar

(121) Batamangala

(122) Kapoteswara

(123) Badadanda

(124) Saradhabali

(125) Muktimandap

(126) Mahodadhi

(127) Swargadwar

Short Account of 127 Sacred centres as shown in respect of their location in the sketch of Sankha kshetra is given below.

Shri Jagannath

This paramount deity is seated on the Ratna Singhasana in the inner most part of the temple. The Lord Jagannath is considered a paramount deity who is one of the Chaturdha Murti. The other Chaturdha Murties which are seated on the Ratna Singhasana by the sides of Lord Jagannath are Shri Balabhadra, Shri Subhadra and Shri Surdarsana who is the Aiyudha of Lord Jagannath. Shri Madhaba is also seated with the holy trinity on the Ratna Singhasana.

Shri Devi-Shri Devi A golden image of Laxmi is also seated on the Ratnavedi at the left side of Lord Jagannath.

Bhu Devi-Bhu Devi which is representative of all powers is also installed on the Ratnavedi.

(1) *Shri Mandir.* Shri Mandir is situated at the navel of Sankha Kshetra. The northern side, southern

side and western side are occupied by three Gopurams including Bamana Murti which is on the southern side, Baraha Murti on the northern side and Nrusimha Murti on the western side of the Gopurams.

Inside the temple on its walls there are many images drawn to add beauty to the temple. But these images which are drawn on the walls are not worshipped. At the apex of the temple a circular object known as *Nilachakra* is present. Flags are hoisted at Nilachakra. A functionary of Chunara caste climbs up to the top of the temple and places a lamp called Mahadipa near Nilachakra on festive occasions.

(2) *Shri Khyetraswari Bimala.* The temple of the goddess Bimala is situated in the south-western corner of the temple. The Bimala temple is within the inner compound called Kurma Bedha. The deity is made up of stone (Black Muguni stone).

(3) *Shri Mahalakshimi.* The temple of goddess Lakshmi is situated on the north-western side of the temple. The image of Lakshmi Nrusimha is installed on the southern side at the entrance of the temple. The images of Mahabir, Haygriba, etc., which are installed at Jagamohan are worshipped. The deity of Lakshmi is of black stone and the deity is decorated with many ornaments including a Mukuta of gold.

(4) *Uttar Durga.* The shrine called uttarayani in which Uttar Durga is installed. It is located on the passage leading to the northern gate. This shrine is also located within inner compound. The image is made of Black stone.

(5) *Bata Mangala.* The temple of Bata Mangala is located under Kalpa Bata. The deity is made of

black stone. A Brahmin worships Bata Mangala and offers fruits and sweet puffed rice.

(6) *Garuda Stamba.* Garuda Stamba is on the eastern side of Jagamohan. This pillar which is of wood is of 10 feet in height. Hundreds of years have passed, but there has been no damage to this wooden pillar. At the top of the pillar the statue of Garuda is installed. The image looks towards the Lord Jagannath and is seated in the form of Jogasana. It is the belief among the people that the water in which the image is bathed cures diseases and removes all difficulties.

(7) *Bhogamandapa.* Bhogamandap is a place, which is situated on the eastern side of Jagamohan. It is called Bhanand house. It was installed when Sankaracharya visited Puri. All types of consecrated foods, which are offered to the deities, are placed at this place. As the quantity of food was not sufficient for a full meal of those who take such Mahaprasad Sankaracharya increased the quantity of the food. As Sankaracharya increased the food, the monasteries that he established at Puri goes by the name Bhogabardhan Math. Later this monastery came to be known as Gobardhan Math. Three functionaries of Puja Panda caste consecrated this food at the place. The consecrated food placed at this Bhanand house is also known as Chatra Bhoga (Public food).

(8) *Kalpa Bata.* Three banyan trees close to each other are present on the western side of Muktimandapa. The Brahmin sebaka offers Puja at these trees. These three tree constituting Kalpa Bata come under sacred centre.

(9) *Rohini Kunda.* Rohini Kunda comprises a micro tank. It is situated in front of Bimala temple. Of the Five tirthas or sacred places Rohini Kunda is

one. Inside the tank there is Surdarsana Chakra one of the Aiyudhas of Vishnu and an image of crow called Bhusanda made of black stone is present. A Brahmin sebaka offers Puja at this place and it comes under sacred place.

(10) *Bata Ganesha.* A mini temple in which Bata Ganesha is situated under Kalpa Bata. The height of the Ganesh is 5 feet and its vehicle is represented by a mouse. This mouse is installed on a small pillar. A Brahmin sebaka offers puja at this place. Sweet balls are favourite of this mouse. This sacred object comes under sacred centres.

(11) *Uchista Ganapati.* The temple of Uchista Ganapati is present on the way leading to the western gate. The image is made up black stone. It is a sacred centre.

(12) *Saraswati.* Goddess Saraswati is installed in a small temple, which is located near the temple of Bhubaneswari, its height is 2 feet and the image is made of stone. A Brahmin worships the goddess and offers dry food.

(13) *Navagraha.* The temple of Navagraha is situated on the northern side of temple of goddess Mahalakhimi. In this temple there are images of Rama, Laxman, Sita and Hanuman. The Goddess Samaleswari is also present in this temple. All the Nine grahas are seated in a line. This temple may come under sacred cluster.

(14) *Konark Surya Deb.* The sun with seven horses of stone is installed in the sun temple, which is called Sun deity of Konark. At this temple there are images of moon and sun which are made up Alloy of eight metals. A Brahmin sebaka worships this

deity. Since there are more than one deity in this temple it comes under sacred cluster. Fruits are offered to the deity

(15) *Pada Padma.* The image representing the feet of Shri Chaitanya Deb are worshipped in a small temple which is located near the path leading to northern gate. The Goudiya Baistambas worships the feet of Shri Chaitanya.

(16) *Jagyambata.* Jagyambata is a sacred tree, which is situated near Jagyam Nrusimha deity. A Brahmin sebakas offers fruits and dry food to this tree. The legend indicates that the tree is there since the Lord Jagannath was installed in the temple.

(17) *Satyanarayana.* The deity Satyanarayan is of black stone. It is installed in a temple, which lies near a Siva temple. The statue faces towards north and comes under sacred centre. A Brahmin sebaka worships the deity.

(18) *Sakhigopinath.* The deity called Sakhigopinath is installed in a small temple, which is located in the inner compound on the western side of Shrimandir. The deity is worshipped along with the image of Radha. The deity Gopinath is made of black stone and Radha is made of brass. The Gajapati Raja Purusottam Dev brought the idol of Sakhi Gopinath by the time of his invasion to Kanchi during the battle between him and the king of Kanchi.

(19) *Jaya Vijaya.* The doorway opening to the Natamandapa is known as Jaya Vijaya (14 feet by 7 feet). Jaya and Vijaya are the celestial creatures of heaven who guard the Ratna

Singhasana. This doorway is one of the finest specimens of Orissan architecture with Sapta Bandha. All aspects of Rashalila of Lord Jagannath have been depicted here. The Oriya inscription during Prataprudra Dev in the (15th century A.D.) Has been inscribed on the side walls of the doorway.

(20) *Agnyeswara.* The Agnyeswara, which is a Siva, is present in a temple, which is located near the passage leading from the temple to the kitchen. The Siva Linga is at a depth of Eight feet from the floor of the temple campus. It is within the inner compound of the temple. It is a sacred centre. The Suara sebakas pay homage first to Agnyeswara Mahadev and after that get into the kitchen room to set fire in the ovens and start cooking the food.

(21) *Indrani (Badreswari).* The goddess Indrani is installed in a temple at the southern side of Shrimandir within its inner compound. The temple is of six feet in height and made of black stone. A Brahmin sebaka offers fruits and dry food to the deity. It comes under sacred centre.

(22) *Khetra Pala.* Khetra Pala is another Siva installed in a small temple located near Muktimandap. This deity is one of the eight Bhairabas, which is mentioned in Tantra Sashtra. A Brahmin worships this deity and offers fruits and dry food.

(23) *Swana Bhairabi.* Swana Bhairabi is located in a temple lying on the southern side of Shrimandir. The wall of this temple shows the image of this deity, which looks like a god. Swana Bhairabi is also called Kutam Chandi.

(24) *Mukteswar.* Mukteswar is a Siva represented by Siva Linga. The deity is installed in a south-facing temple near Muktimandapa. A Brahmin Sebaka offers fruits.

(25) *Ghorakali.* Ghorakali is a deity which is installed in a small temple near Muktimandapa the deity is of black stone. Fruits and dry food are offered to the deity everyday by a Brahmin sebaka.

(26) *Bata Markandeswara.* Bata Markandeswara is one of the five Sivas, which are present in the inner compound of Shrimandir. As the deity is present at the root of the Bata Vrikhya the deity is called Bata Markandeswara. The temple of Bata Markandeswara is two feet in height. The Linga representing the deity is at a depth of seven feet below the surface. A Rishi named Markanda lived long by worshipping this Siva deity and therefore the deity is known as Bata Markandeswara. The image of Markanda Rushi and Markandeswar Siva figures adorn the wall of the temple. The Brahmin sebaka worships the deity

(27) *Katyayani Budhima.* Katyayani Budhima is a deity, which is installed in a small temple, which is located on the passage leading from the temple to the southern gate. The temple is present on a high platform. A Brahmin sebaka worships the deity and offers fruits and dry foods. The people worship the deity in order to be free from smallpox.

(28) *Gopeswaram.* Gopeswara is a Siva, which is installed in a temple lying on the western side of the Shrimandir close to inner compound wall. Inside the temple there are some other deities namely Purnamasi, Gopi Gopala, Dhenu Bachha,

Nanda, Josada etc. which are present on a platform inside the temple. One small image representing Patitapaban is worshipped at this place. Dry food and fruits are offered by a Brahmin sebaka.

(29) *Bedha Kali.* The temple of Bedha Kali is located on the western side of Shrimandir close to the compound wall. The statue of the deity is of stone. A Brahmin sebaka worships this deity.

(30) *Pataleswari.* Pataleswari is installed in a small temple at the northern side of the temple on the way leading to northern gate. The Linga representing Pataleswara lies at a depth of 12 feet from the floor of the temple. A Brahmin Sebaka offers fruits and dry food to the deity.

(31) *Bhubaneswari.* Bhubaneswari is installed in a temple, which is situated on the western side in the inner compound. Some people refer this goddess as Kamala. The statue is made of Black stone and is five feet in height. She is ornamented with silver ornaments. A Brahmin sebaka offers dry food and fruits.

(32) *Baikunthaswara.* Baikunthaswara is installed in a Siva temple located in the north-eastern corner of the inner compound. A Brahmin sebaka offers fruits and dry food. Since the Linga of this deity belongs to the area called Koili Baikuntha its name has been Baikunthaswara.

(33) *Jagyeswari.* Jagyeswari is installed in a Siva temple located in a temple in the inner compound.

(34) *Aisanyeswara.* Aisanyeswara is installed in a Siva temple, which is located at the eastern side of the entrance, which is, called Hastidwara. The

deity is present inside a deep hole. A Brahmin sebaka offers fruits and flowers to the deity at this sacred centre.

(35) *Shitala.* The image of Shitala is situated on the southern side near the well, which is called Golden well. A Brahmin offers dry food and fruits and the public worships the deity because it is the belief that the deity cures smallpox. It comes under sacred centre.

(36) *Bhetamandapa.* Bhetamandapa of an elevated platform is situated at a distance of 25 feet upward from the 1st step of the Baisipahacha or 22 steps. On the way leading to inner compound when Jagannath and Subhadra and Balabhadra return during car festival they wait at this place where goddess Laxhimi receives them and escorts them to the place where they are seated on Ratnavedi.

(37) *Pakasala.* The temple kitchen is located on the southern-eastern part of the temple. It is a very big building having space inside, for cooking consecrated foods, which are offered to the deity. This building is located on an elevated place. Many Brahmins of Supakar category and the Mahanta of different monasteries prepare foods at this place. The ovens are distributed among the Supakar sebakas who have rights to sale or buy these ovens. The public is prohibited to enter the kitchen and it comes under sacred centre.

(38) *Dakhineswari.* Dakhineswari is installed in a small temple, which is located on the right side of the kitchen. The deity called Shri Sadasiba represented by a small Linga. A Brahmin sebaka offers fruits and dry foods.

(39) *Kundaleswara.* Kundaleswara is installed in a small temple near the temple in which Dakhinaswari is installed. A Brahmin sebaka worships the deity and offers dry food and fruits.

(40) *Gouranga.* The temple belonging to Gouranga is located on the way to the temple through the southern entrance. Gouranga, which is a very big statue, is decorated in a very beautiful manner. Particularly the Bengali pilgrims gather here and pay homage to the deity. It is a sacred centre of Goudiya Baistamb sect.

(41) *Sri Ram.* Sri Ram temple is located on the passage leading towards southern gate. In this temple Sri Ram, Laxman and Sita are worshipped. A Brahmin worships the deities and offers food. A great festival is observed at this place on Ram Nabami.

(42) *Barabhai Hanuman.* A deity called Barabhai Hanuman is worshipped at the place leading towards southern gate. The deity is installed in a temple along with the main deity in which there are images of 12 Hanumans. These Hanumans have different names such as Janma Hanuman, Gaya Hanuman, Gabakhya, Sukhena, Bada Hanuman, Tarakhya, Jambabana, Angada, Sauri, Sugriba, and Nanda, Nilla. The Brahmin sebaka offers special food the Banana and coconut.

(43) *Nirmalya Hanuman.* Having five heads is installed in a small temple located in the flower garden in the outer compound of the temple. The statue is made of stone and four feet in height. It is at this place that cooked rice is spread on a platform to dry them.

(44) *Upabana Alakabatica.* This is a garden of flowers which is located at the south-western corner of the temple. It also has many Tulsi trees. The flowers collected from this garden are offered to the deities.

(45) *Rameswar.* The temple of Rameswar is on the western side in the outer compound of the temple. The Linga of the deity is of small height.

(46) *Chakra Narayan.* The Lord Narayana is present within a circle near Rameswar temple. A Brahmin worships the deity.

(47) *Chaturdham.* The deity known as Chaturdham worshipped in a small temple is located near the passage leading to western gate. The deities, which are placed side by side inside the temple, are Jagannath, Ramnath, Dwarikanath and Bhadrinath. A Brahmin sebaka worships the deities and offers fruits and dried food.

(48) *Kanpata Hanuman.* The temple in which the deity called Kanpata Hanuman is located near the passage leading to western gate. The image of the deity is of six feet in height. People worship the deity in order to get well at the time of their illness. In the south-facing temple the east-facing statue is installed. The hanuman is called Sankata Mochana Hanuman because it protects the people at the time of their difficulties. This deity has divine power to control the sound from the sea so that other deities present in the temple are not disturbed. A Brahmin worships the deity.

(49) *Niladri Bihar.* Niladri Bihar is located near the temple in which Kanpata Hanuman is installed. The place consists of eight rooms. Different

images of god are kept in the boxes made of glass. The pilgrims visit this place at the time of their pilgrimage. Tickets have to be purchased in order to get into the rooms to see the images of the God. At the door of this place there is a statue of Lord, which is of eight feet in height. The images are made of earth, which is painted, with different colours.

(50) *Bayubyeswara.* The deity is a Siva installed in a temple and indicated in the Sankha Kshetra under No. 50.

(51) *Adagdha Sialilata.* Adagdha Sialilata is confined to the area of Koili Baikuntha in the outer compound of the temple. This place has many plants. It is so to say a flower garden. This place has a pit of five feet in depth and 30 feet in length. It is in this pit that the old images of the three deities are buried at the time of Nabakalebara. The pilgrims are required to pay a fee to go inside this garden.

(52) *Koili Baikuntha.* This place is located in the outer compound of the temple. It is on the northern side of the temple. At this place there are images of Hanuman and Garuda. A big hall in which the images of Galumadhaba and Indradyumna etc. are present. These images are made of cement.

(53) *Tapaswi Hanuman.* Tapaswi Hanuman is installed near the passage leading to the northern gate. The deities are carried to pass through the Hanuman while taking them to Koili Baikuntha for burial. Many bats hang themselves from the ailing of the northern entrance room.

(54) *Subarna Kupa.* The well which is present on the passage leading to northern gate is called the golden well from which 108 pitchers of water are taken for the ceremonial bath of Lord Jagannath during the Snana Yatra.

(55) *Ananda Bazar Kaiblya.* Ananda Bazar Kaiblya is a very big open space lying on the northern side in the outer compound of the temple, where Mahaprasada is sold daily, to the public. There are small sweet stalls around the place. Those sweets are all consecrated food, which were offered to the deities before. Previously the consecrated foods were being sold on the place comprising 22 steps, which lead to the main temple.

(56) *Devasnana Mandapa.* On the eastern side of the Ananda Bazar there is the Devasnana Mandapa where the deities are ceremonially bathed on the full-moon day of Jaistha (May-June).

(57) *Chahani Mandapa.* Close to the Devasnana Mandapa there is a small pavilion where the goddess Lakshmi takes her seat to see the Snana yatra. There is a corresponding pavilion on the other side of the eastern gateway to which Lakshmi resorts to welcome Jagannath on his return from Gundicha Ghara during the Car festival.

(58) *Baisipahacha.* There are 22 flights of steps (Baisipahacha) from the eastern gateway of the outer enclosure. The width of the middle 15 steps varies from 5 feet 10 half inches to 6 feet 3 inches and the height of 6 inches to 7 inches. The size of the remaining steps is smaller both in length and width. The steps are made of feldspar and Khondalite.

(59) *Kashi Biswanath.* The idols of Kashi Biswanath, Ramachandra, Nrusimha, and Ganesh have been installed on the southern side of the Baisipahacha.

(60) *Phate Hanuman.* Phate Hanuman is installed close to the lion's gate. A Brahmin offers dry food and fruits. The deity is worshipped by the people in order to be successful in their work.

(61) *Patitapabana.* The image of Patitapabana is situated on the northern side of the lion gate. Formerly the untouchables who were not allowed to go inside the temple used to offer their prayers to Patitapabana (Jagannath) by standing outside the temple. In front of the Patitapabana a small image of Garuda has been installed.

(62) *Simhadwara.* The eastern entrance of the outer enclosure is called Simhadwara or the Lion's gate. The image of Nabagraha and Mahalaxmis are installed at the top of the gate.

(63) *Meghanada Pacheri.* The temple has two big compound walls and four gates both in outer and inner walls. The outer wall of the temple is known as Meghanada Pacheri (665 ft. x 640 ft.). The height of the outer wall varies from 20 ft. to 24 ft. There is no historical evidence to prove when the outer wall was constructed. But from the Madala Panji and the local tradition it is known that these were built not earlier than the 15th century A.D.

(64) *Badachhata Matha.* Badachhata Math is a monastery associated with the temple. It is Matha of Ramanandi sect (Sampradaya).

(65) *Uttar Dwara (Hastidwara).* The Hastidwara or the Elephant Gate had on each side a colossal figure of elephant, which is said to have been disfigured during the Muslim invasion. Subsequently these

elephants were repaired and plastered, and placed at the northern gate of the inner enclosure (Kurma Bedha). The inner enclosure is approached by thirteen flights of steps made of Khondalite, from the northern gateway of the outer enclosure. The deities of Lokanath, uttarani, Lakshimi-Nrusimha, Baraha and Sitala have been installed in the outer enclosure. Near the gate of the Murma Bedha, stands a banian tree; During the Nabakalebara, the images of Jagannath, Balabhadra and Subhadra are being shaped here.

(66) *Paschima Dwara (Vyaghradwara, Western Gate).* The Vyaghradwara or the Tiger gate has on each side a statue of a tiger made of mortar. The inner enclosure is approached by seven flights of steps, made of Khondalite, from the western gateway of the outer enclosure. The deities of Rameswar-Mahadeva, Sri Jagannath, Dwarakanath, and Badrinath are installed in the outer enclosure in a shrine known as Chaturdham. Flower gardens have been set up on both the sides from which flowers are collected for the daily worship of the deities. The shrines of Chakranayarana, Sidheswara, Mahabir Hanuman and Dhabaleswar Mahadeva are located in this area.

(67) *Mangaleswari.* It is a female deity worshipped on certain special occasions.

(68) *Durgamadhaba.* Durgamadhaba is a deity having image of Durga and that Madhaba in combination. It is worshipped on special occasions.

(69) *Dakhina Dwara (Aswa Dwara).* The Aswadwara or the Horse Gate has on each side a galloping stallion of masonry work with the figures of

Jagannath and Balabhadra on their back in full military array. These sculptures depict the legendary Kanchi expedition of Jagannath and Balabhadra, and have been installed recently. The inner enclosure is approached by ten flights of steps, made of Khondalite, from the southern gateway of the outer enclosure. The images of Sadhabhuja Gouranga, Ramachandra, Gopala, Barabhai Hanuman and Nrusimha have been installed in small shrines in the outer enclosure.

(70) *Prahari Hanuman.* Prahari Hanuman is installed in the passage leading ιo kitchen. The deity is south facing and of six feet in height. Since the deity watches the incoming and outgoing persons through this passage the deity is named as per his duty. A Brahmin offers dry food and fruits and worships the deity.

(71) *Chhauni Math.* It is monastery associated with the temple.

(72) *Aruna Stamba.* It is a monastery associated with the temple's eastern gateway and there is the beautiful sun pillar which originally stood before the sun temple at Konark. It was shifted to this place by the Marathas. The sun pillar is a monolithic shaft of chlorite with sixteen sides. It is 25 feet, and two inches in height, two feet in diametre and six feet and 3 half inches in circumference. On the top of the sun pillar the image of Arun (Sun God) is seated in the form of Jogasana. A sebaka of Chunara caste worships this pillar.

(73) *Jagannath Ballava.* It is a monastery intimately associate with the temple.

(74) *Narendra Puskarani (Tank).* The Narendra tank is situated about a mile from the Jagannath temple and covers an area of over 3.240 hectares (8 acres). It is 834 feet by 873 feet in size. The tank has an island in its middle bearing a small temple connected with the south bank by means of a bridge, to which Madana Mohan, the representative deity of Jagannath, is brought for 21 days during the Chandan Yatra (April-May). Every afternoon during the Yatra the God Madan Mohan is moved around in a boat in the tank amidst public visitors.

(75) *Bisweswari.* The deity is a Siva worshipped on special occasions.

(76) *Dolabedi.* Dolabedi is a huge platform decorated with various designs around it. It is located outside the temple compound. The mobile representatives of the deities are brought from the temple and are made to swing at this place on the fullmoon day in the month of Phalguna. The devices, which are used, for the swing are fixed in the structure called Torona which is made of black stone.

(77) *Makardhwaja Hanuman.* The side of the way leading from Atharanala to Puri town installs Makardhwaja Hanuman

(78) *Alamba Devi or Alam Chandi.* Alam chandi is present at the entrance to the Puri town near the bridge called Atharanala when the logs of wood are brought to Puri during Nabakalebara. The cartloads of logs are brought into Puri through the place where Alam chandi is placed. It is the belief that Alam chandi is supreme to sanctify the logs so that no harm is done at the time shaping them to form the figures of the three deities.

(79) *Atharanala.* The Atharanala Bridge, which crosses the Madhupur stream, measures in all two hundred and ninety feet long and is composed of eighteen passages through which water flows down. It is built of laterite and sandstones. The bridge is said to have been built towards the end of the 13th century A.D. and is mentioned in Chaitanya's biography (16th century) and William Bruton's travels (1633).

(80) *Bhargabi Nadi.* It is a river which flows on the northern side of Sankha Kshetra. This is a sacred river from which water is collected by the devotees of Lord Siva called Shri Lokanath to bathe the deity with this water. The famous Kopoteswar Siva is worshipped near this river.

(81) *Saptamatruka.* At the northern ghat under a fig tree (*Ficus indicus*) are placed eight stone images each four feet high representing the Astamatrukas or the eight sacred mothers, who are sisters to each other.

(82) *Markanda Pokhari (Tank).* Markanda Tank is situated about 3 furlongs to the north of the Jagannath temple and is lined throughout with stones covering an area of nearly four acres. It is irregular in shape. It has several ghats around it with a Siva temple (Markandeswar temple) on the south side and is visited by the pilgrims. Its sides measure 350 on the northern side 508 on the eastern side 385 feet on the southern side, 542 feet on the western side. At the northern ghat under a fig tree (Ficus indicus) are placed eight stone images each four feet high representing the Astamatrukas or the eight sacred mothers.

(83) *Markandeswara.* A Siva temple which is located on the south side of the Markanda Tank, The Brahmin sebaka worships this deity.

(84) *Bhagabati.* It is a female deity worshipped on special occasions.

(85) *Banadurga.* Banadurga is a goddess, which is located in Manikarnika Street. During Dasara festival non-vegetarian food is offered to the deity. A Brahmin worships the deity and offers dry food and fruits.

(86) *Ghatamangala.* Ghatamangala is present in a place called *Mangala ghat* on the road leading from Puri to brahmagiri. Pilgrims while going to Brahmagiri pass through the place where Ghatamangala is installed. There was a river called Mangala River, which was flowing along this road, and the pilgrims have to cross this river while going to Brahmagiri.

(87) *Chamundeswari.* Goddess is present in Manikarnika Street, when there is epidemic of smallpox they worship this goddess in order to be free from the disease. A Brahmin worships the deity and offers fruits and dry food.

(88) *Harachandi.* Harachandi is a goddess installed in the Harachandi Street.

(89) *Pandu Ashram.* Pandu Ashram is located in Harachandi Street near the temple of Jambeswar. It was established by a Rishi and according to his name this Ashram is called Pandu Ashram.

(90) *Nikumbhila Bata.* It is a garden which is visited by the pilgrims.

(91) *Kandu Ashram.* Kandu Ashram is located at the end of the Harachandi Street, near Jambeswar temple. It is one kilometre distance from Shrimandir. It was established by a Risi and

according to his name this Ashram is called Kandu Ashram.

(92) *Parvati Sagar*. It is a sacred tank which is located on the northern side of Shri Lokanath temple. It is here where the children are shaven for the first time to offer their hair to the deity, on festive occasion. The devotees light lamp all around this tank and take bath.

(93) *Sri Lokanath*. The Lokanath temple is situated about 3 kilometres away from the Jagannath temple on the western outskirts of the town. Its presiding deity Lokanath, a Linga, remains always under water in a small square pit fed by a natural spring of the near-by Parvati tank. On the night of Sivaratri, all the water is bailed out to make the Linga visible to the worshippers. The god Lokanath is highly esteemed by the people. The tank contains several small tortoises.

(94) *Yameswara*. At a distance of about half a mile (804.672 metres) to the south of the Jagannath temple, in the Gaudabada Sahi, Yameswara is a small temple of little architectural importance.

(95) *Baseli*. Baseli or Adanga Baseli the temple of the deity is located on south-western side of the temple outside Meghanada Pacheri. A part of the main temple was connected with the temple long back and therefore it is called Adanga (Varendha) baseli. The temple is at a height of 35 feet above the road level.

(96) *Kapapalmochan*. Kapalamochan is a small Siva temple in the immediate neighbourhood of the Albukeswara Siva deity in the Manikarnika sahi. The sacred pool of Manikarnika is also losivacated here.

(97) *Manikarnika (Pool).* Manikarnika pool is a sacred place located in the street called Manikarnika. The pilgrims during their visit to Puri take bath in this pool. It is a sacred pool of Puri.

(98) *Barahi Devi.* The goddess called Barahi is installed in a temple, which is located in the middle of the Bali Street. It is known as a centre of Tantra activities. Some consecrated food such as sweet is offered to the deity everyday. It has connections with the temple. Since the offerings are supplied from the temple it is a sacred centre.

(99) *Shyama Kali.* The goddess Shyama Kali is installed in a temple, which is located in Bali Sahi. Formerly the goddess was the presiding deity of Gajapati Rajas and therefore the temple was within the premises of Rajpalace at Bali Sahi. After Gajapati Raja shifted from Bali sahi to grand road the goddess is left behind without care. Therefore the people of Bali sahi have taken up the responsibility of taking care of the goddess and offering food and other materials in festivities.

(100) *Sankarcharya Math.* Sankaracharya Math was established by Sankarcharya during his visit to Puri sometime in 8th century. The Math is now known as Bhogabardhan Math or Gobardhan Math. Sankarcharya was preaching Brahminic tradition and his disciples were in charge of imparting training to the ritual functionaries in the matter of worship of Lord Jagannath. Sankarcharya was very much associated with the Jagannath temple and was so to say a guardian of Jagannath cult and tradition.

(101) *Mukti Shala.* Mukti Shala a sacred place located near Sweta Ganga. The pilgrims visit this place

during their ceremonial bath in the Sweta Ganga tank, which is one of the five famous pilgrim centres.

(102) *Swetaganga.* Swetaganga is a small tank, to the west of the Jagannath temple. On its bank there are two small temples, one dedicated to Sweta Madhava and the other to Matsya madhava, both forming the Vishnu cult. It is here that the people perform Sradha ceremony.

(103) *Ugreswara Ashram.* This place is located in Bali sahi close to Swetaganga tank. The image of Ugreswar is located near Bhrugu Ashram. The temple of Ugreswar comes under sacred centre.

(104) *Dakhina Kali.* The goddess Dakhina Kali is installed in a temple in Kalika Devi Street. The deity is made of black stone and is worshipped by the people of Kalika Devi Street. The deity is 1 half feet in height having four heads and three eyes. The tradition is that even the Lord Jagannath is considered Dakhina Kali. What mentioned in the text of Maha Tantra Sastra is reproduced below:

"Ugratara Sulapani Subhadra Bhubaneswari Niladrou Tu Jagannath Sakhyata Dhakhina Kalika".

(105) *Siddha Bakula Math.* The monastery is located in Bali sahi. There is a tree of Barala Bakul tree of five hundred years old. The peculiarity of this tree is that it has no trunk (Gandi) or body. The tree is originated from the bark only. As a saint named Thakura Haridas used to recite the names of God and in deep meditation at the root of this tree and finally got the blessings of the God accordingly the monastery is called Sidha Bakula Math. It is

here that a temple of Haridas is present. There are many other deities such as Gouranga, patitapabana, Radha Krushna, and many Salagramas worshipped in the compound of the monastery. The Vaishnabas of Gouranga sect perform seba puja in this place. More than one deity is worshipped in this place and therefore this place comes under a sacred cluster.

(106) *Narayani.* Narayani temple is located in Dolamandapa sahi of Puri. A festival called Sarata Gundichais performed at this place. The Puja of Durga Madhaba is performed at this temple for a period of eight days during Durga Puja, which last for 16 days.

(107) *Sodasaputri.* A goddess is known as Sodasaputri is worshipped in Dolomandap sahi. The deity is installed in a temple and of 5 feet in height and made of black stone. Dry food and sweets are offered to the deity.

(108) *Marichika.* The goddess called Marichika is installed in a temple, which is located in the grand road near Marichikot crussing. The deity is worshipped during Durga Puja. The goddess called Kanaka Durga, which is installed in the compound of the palace of the Gajapati Raja, is brought to the place where Marichika Goddess is installed to take part in the Puja, which is performed at this place during Durga Puja. It is a sacred centre.

(109) *Charchika Devi.* The temple in which the goddess Charchika is installed in located in the grand road near temple office of Puri, Jagannath temple. It was the tradition that when the Gajapati Rajas used to go out on an invasion to fight against their

enemies they used to come to this place where Charchika Goddess is installed and offer worship and prayer to have success in their battle. The carpenters and others who are engaged in the construction of the cars offer worship at this place. The administrative staff of the temple office meets the expenses of food and sweets offered to the deity.

(110) *Ardhasani.* On the way to Gundicha temple, Ardhasani temple is present. She is also known as Mausi Maa (mother's sister) of Lord Jagannath. It is a sacred centre.

(111) *Daria Hanuman.* At a distance of about thirty metres to the west of the Chakra Narayan temple, Daria Mahabir is installed in a small temple dedicated to Hanuman. He is also known as Bedi Hanuman. It is a sacred centre.

(112) *Chakra Narayan.* Towards the northern side of the temple of Sunar-Gouranga is the temple of Chakranarayan. The image of Lakshmi Narasimha is worshipped here. It is a sacred centre.

(113) *Chakra Tirtha.* The Chakratirtha, a small and unprotected pool, is in the eastern side of Puri beach where pilgrims come to perform Sradha. It is evidently a part of the old mouth of the Balagandi stream that flowed across the Badadanda to the sea. The place is also known as Bankimuhana. Near-by is the temple of Chaitanya called Sunar-Gouranga, a place largely visited by the pilgrims.

(114) *Sri Gundicha Mandir.* Gundicha temple is the most important sanctuary of Lord Jagannath. The

cars are drawn to this place during car festival and the deities Balabhadra, Subhadra, and Jagannath are brought inside and are seated on the Singhasana (Ratnavedi). The deities are kept here for nine days after which they are brought back to the temple. The Gundichaghar is situated at the end of the (Badadanda), the distance between the Jagannath temple and the Gundicha temple, is about two kms. The temple is surrounded by a wall and stands in the middle of a garden. It consists of four parts connected with kitchen rooms by a narrow passage. The temple is 75 feet high with a base of 55 feet by 46 feet.

(115) *Adi Nrusimha Nath.* The temple in which the deity Adi Nrusimhanath is installed is located close to the Gundicha temple. The tradition says that Indradyumna constructed the Nrusimhanath temple. The deity is said to have intimate relationship with Lord Jagannath and other deities of the temple. The bullock cart in which the logs of wood required for the construction of the cars are brought along the road leading to the temple of Nrusinhanath.

(116) *Nilakantheswar.* Shri Nilakantheswar is one of the famous Siva of Puri. The temple of Lord Siva is located near the Indradyumna tank. Padma Keshari of Keshari dynasty has constructed this temple. The Nilakantheswar is one of the Five famous Siva deities of Puri.

(117) *Indradyumna Tank.* The Indradyumna tank is situated to the north-east of Gundicha temple and contains good water. It is 396 feet wide and 485 feet long, and covers an area of four and half acres. It is said that Indradyumna is most sacred of all the tirthas of Puri. In contained several big old

tortoises, which came ashore to take offered by the pilgrims. The whereabouts of these tortoises are not known. Tradition has it that the labourers who carried stone for the construction of great temple were, because of hard work, turned into tortoises and remained here ever since. On the south-west bank of the tank is the temple of Nilakantheswara. It is a sacred centre.

(118) *Siddha Hanuman.* At a distance of about half a mile to the west of Gundicha temple, there is a small temple dedicated to Siddha Hanuman. It is believed that Tulasidas resided at this place during his stay at Puri. It is a beautiful, spot for picnic.

(119) *Beleswar.* The Sivalinga of Beleswar temple is at a depth of 22ft. from the ground floor. It comes under sacred cluster.

(120) *Mukteswar.* Mukteswara is a famous Siva temple of Puri. This temple is located in a prominent place of Srikshetra. During pilgrimage to Puri many pilgrims visit the place to worship the Siva. Formerly there was no temple of Muktesvar who was installed in an open place under the sky. Therefore, the name Mukteswara is given to the deity.

(121) *Bata Mangala.* The temple of goddess Bata Mangala is located by the side of Puriroad at a distance of about five Kilometres from Puri town.

(122) *Kopoteswara.* The Siva linga of Kopoteswara lies at a depth of 7 feet from ground floor. It comes under sacred cluster.

(123) *Badadanda.* The main road of the town, called Badadanda, is a very wide road used for the journey of the Lords during the famous Car

Festival. It extends from the Gundicha temple to the eastern gate (Simhadwara) of Jagannath temple, the exact distance being 2688,0696 metres (8.326 ft). The streets spread out somewhat in the shape of a fan with Badadanda as its handle. The Badadanda has only a few residential quarters, It is crowded mainly by shops, lodging houses, Dharmasalas, Mathas, and a few public buildings including the Town Police Station and the hospital. The palace of the Raja of Puri built in 1918 is also located on the Badadanda.

(124) *Saradhabali.* The area of Badadanda in its midway is called Saradhabali. Formerly a river was flowing in this place cutting across the grand road but there is no trace of this river today.

(125) *Muktimandap.* Muktimandapa is a structure, which is present in front of the southern side of the main temple. It is also known as Brahmasava. It is a rectangular building, 38 feet square, with a plain high plinth and a pyramidal roof supported on sixteen massive chlorite pillars. It is said to have been erected by Prataprudra Dev in 1525 A.D. On the floor of this mandapa the Sanyasis of Sankara Math and sixteen pandits belonging to the sixteen sasans established by the kings of Orissa, are allowed to sit and take part in learned discourses. It is under sacred centre.

(126) *Mahodadhi (the sea).* Mohodadhi is located one kilometre distance from Shrimandir towards south. The beach of Mahodadhi is always crowded in the morning and evening. It is largely frequented by bathers, especially in the month of Kartika. On the full-moon day of Kartika (October-November) thousands of people come here to bathe. In *Skandha Purana* the sea is designated as

Mohadadhi (the great sea), which is also called Bay of Bengal. The sea is one of its main Five Tirthas.

(127) *Swargadwara.* The Swargadwara, or the gateway to heaven, is in the sandy beach towards the south-western corner of the town. It is said to be the place where God at the invitation of King Indradyumna came down to consecrates the sacred images. A dip in the sea near it is believed to secure heavenly bliss. When men die in such a place they enjoy an easy path to heaven.

The descriptive account of these sacred places particularly the geographical location of certain temple shows that some temples are located much below the present ground level. In some cases the temples are seen at a depth of about 40-ft. above the ground level. As against this the compound of the Jagannath temple are found much above the ground level. It means that some sacred centres are below the sea level and some above the sea level. Such uneven location of the sacred centres leads to take up a study on the historical geography of Puri town. Such a study which refers to the Historical Geography means that a geographical study of the history of changing territorial boundaries and levels of different places resulting from the administrative divisions on account of political change on the one hand and on account of the influences of geographic factors on the other. A probe into this matter requires a separate study for which further time and necessary financial aid are needed. There is no scope for such studies on historical geography under the present study on the Sacred Geography of Puri.

(D) Important Sacred Places

Besides the Jagannath temples many other shrines located around the temple within the inner compound

(Kuruma bedha) there are many other sacred places in and around Puri town and immediate suburbs of the town. Some such important sacred places are the temples of the eight Sambhus, and eight Saktis (Chandis) and four sacred tanks. The eight guardians Sivas of the abode of Vishnu are Markendaswar, Yajneswara, Nilakanthaswar, Vilviswara, Kapalamochana, Beleswar, Isaneswara and Pateleswara. The eight Chandis are Batamangala, Bimala, Sarvamangala, Ardhasini, Alamba, Dakhinakalika, Marichika, and Harachandi, The sacred tanks are Indradyumna, Manikarnika, Markanda, Swetaganga. These four tirthas or sacred water with the sea make the Panchatirtha. A few other places such as the Narendra tank, Swargadwara, Chakratirtha, Lokanath Siva temple, Atharanala bridge, are also equally sacred which the pilgrims circumambulate. All these sacred temples, sites, places, tanks and the sea are all included in the Sankha Kshetra which comprise the subject matter of the study under the Research Project namely the Sacred Geography of Puri.

The Jegagharas, which are the old socio religious and cultural institutions, form special features of Puri town. The Jegagharas have each a house of its own situated in different localities or sahis of the town where people assemble for recreation and for gymnastic performances. Some deities particularly hanuman are worshipped in the Jegagharas and these institutions play a prominent role in the important festivals observed in the town including the temple of Lord Jagannath. Some of the Jegagharas of Puri town are Marichakot Jaga, Ganesh Guruja, Kadambagarh, Brahmi Jaga, Guru Jang, Nuagarh, Sankat Mazena Mallah, Satabakhara, Sundara, Mali, Visuni, Panda, Bhogo, Duari, Gopal tirtha, Panchuati, Champagarh, Khuntia, Tapanga and Birabati. Each of these Jegagharas performs specific festivals on different occasions in honour of the Lord Jagannath.

Puri functions not only as a sacred place to be visited by thousands of pilgrims from all over the country but it also serves as a holiday resort. With the opening of the railways in 1901 travel to Puri has become easier and both Europeans and Indians visit Puri in large number particularly in summer. The Jagannath road, which is now metalled, has made the journey to Puri much easier. Bathing in the sea is enjoyable, as it is one of the best beaches in the eastern seashore. In every hotel there are trained swimmers (*Nulias*) with typical conical straw caps to help visitors to go out into the sea. Thus Puri is not only a famous place of pilgrimage but it is also a place giving enjoyment for a sea bath and walking in the seashore and as a place serving as a health resort.

The Sankha Kshetra consists of Seven folds (*Saptabharana*) each fold starting from inner most folds to the outermost fold comprises many sacred places. Shrines temples, tanks, monasteries and some other sacred spots. There are 127 sacred places in the Map of Sankha Kshetra where as there are only 60 sacred places mentioned in different folds. The list of sacred places present in the Map of Sankha Kshetra and those of seven folds is given below. The detailed account of all these sacred places of both of the folds and of the Map is presented below:

Present in fold	*Present in Map*
	First Fold
Shri Kshetra	Shri Kshetra
	Second Fold
Bimala	2 Bimala
Kamala	-
Sarbamangala	-
Utarayani	-

Present in fold	*Present in Map*
Kalpabata	8 Kalpabata
Salmalitaru	
Rohini Kuṇda	9 Rohini Kunda
Pranitodaka Kunda (Suna Kua)	54 Subarna Kupa
Third Fold	
Agneswar	20 Agneswar
Bateswar	-
Kshetrapaleswar	22 Kshetrapala
Chakraswar	-
Baikuntheswar	-
Pateleswar	30 Pataleswari
Isaneswar	34 Isaneswar
Lokeswar	-
Dwarabasini	-
Mahabajreswari	-
Swanbhairabi	23 Swanbhairabi
Vadrekali	-
Bhubaneswari	Bhubaneswari
Mahakaliaghorea	-
Sitala	35 Sitala
Jagnyeswari	33 Jagnyaeswari
Fourth Fold	
Mahakurma	-
Inner Compound wall	-

Present in fold	*Present in Map*
Fifth Fold	
Bisweswara	-
Markendaswar	83 Markendaswar
Mahakaleswar	-
Karnameswar	-
Mukteswar	24 Mukteswar
Ugreswar	103 Ugreswar Ashram
Kapala Mochana	-
Agreswar	-
Bisweswari	75 Bisweswari
Saptamatruka	81 Saptamatruka
Dakhinakali	104 Dakhinakali
Charchika	109 Charchika
Alameswari	
Barahi	98 Barahi
Bana Durgeswari	85 Banadurga
Basulikeswari	-
Sixth Fold	
Manikarnika	97 Manikarnika
Swetaganga	102 Swetaganga
Indradyumna	117 Indradyumna
Markendaswar	82 Markendeswar
Mahodadhi	126 Mohodadhi

Present in fold	*Present in Map*
Angira	
Pandu	89 Pandu ashram
Markendiya	-
Bhrigu	-
	Seventh Fold
Nilakantheswar	16 Nilakantheswar
Narasingha	115 Adi Nrusinhanath
Ardhasosani	110 Ardhasosani Mausima
Bilweswar	119 Bilweswar
Lokeswar	-
Kapileswar	-
Chakratirtha	113 Chakratirtha
Swargadwara	127 Swargadwara

Sacred places present in Map as indicated under numbers given below:

1, 3, 4, 5, 6, 7, 10, 11, 12, 13, 14, 15, 16, 17, 18, 19, 21, 25, 26, 27, 28, 29, 36, 37, 38, 39, 40, 41, 42, 43, 44, 45, 46, 47, 48, 49, 50, 51, 52, 53, 55, 56, 57, 58, 59, 60, 61, 62, 63, 64, 65, 66, 67, 68, 69, 70, 71, 72, 73, 74, 76, 77, 78, 79, 80, 84, 86, 87, 88, 90, 91, 92, 93, 94, 95, 96, 99, 100, 101, 105, 106, 107, 108, 111, 112, 114, 118, 121, 122, 123, 124, 125.

Total No. as per Map	-	127
Total No. as per fold	-	60
Lacking in fold	-	67

Structural Significance by folds of Sankha Kshetra

1st fold	-	Innermost, Naval, or Kshetra
2nd fold	-	Outer layer of 1st fold
3rd fold	-	Outer layer of 2nd fold
4th fold	-	Outer coating of 3rd fold
5th fold	-	Outer layer of 4th fold
6th fold	-	Outer layer of 5th fold
7th fold	-	Outer most zones consisting of sentries of Sankha Kshetra and two pilgrim centers.

A list of sacred places within the Jagannath Temple are given in Annexure-3.

7

Findings and Conclusion

Puri is a small town (population 125199 as per 1991 census) situated on the east seacoast of Bay of Bengal in Orissa. It is the headquarters of Puri district. It lies in $19^{0}48'$N and $85^{0}40'$ E. It is a famous pilgrim centre being the abode of the famous paramount deity of Lord Jagannath, the Lord of the Universe. The pilgrims from far off places and from the near by places come to Puri in lakhs to witness the Car festival as well as some other festivals observed at Puri. It is about 311 miles from Calcutta and 572 miles from Banaras by railway. Towards the latter part of the year 1918 the Howrah-Puri express train was introduced reducing the journey time to 12 hours. Moreover the Jagannath road which came up in early 19th century connected Puri with Howrah making it convenient to the pilgrims to come to Puri in large number. Puri is described by those who live in it in the following words.

It is to India what Jerusalem was to the whole land of Israel. It is the Holy Land of the Hindus. As the Israelites go up to worship at Mount Zion, so do the inhabitants of the various parts of India go on pilgrimage to the great temple of Lord Jagannath. The very ground around Puri for ten miles is to the Hindu mind of such sanctity as to absolve from the deepest sin all who proceed thither. The priests of Lord Jagannath speak of it as the city of heaven upon earth. They say that the fruit of the trees there is as the fruit of the tree of life, that the tanks contain the waters of immortality, that to bathe in them is far more meritorious than to bathe in all the sacred rivers of India, that the people are all holy, that the goddess of Fortune resides there, that pilgrims may actually eat of food cooked with her own hands, that the gods of heaven over and anon send showers of beautiful scented flowers upon the city, that all the celestial deities would delight to become incarnate there, that the very dust of the city is pure gold and that the great idol is so mighty and gracious that he pardons the sins of those who may have killed a million Brahmans.*

Puri is known by various names of which Sankha Kshetra is one. It is named so because the sacred part of Puri looks like a conch shell and it is in this part that all the sacred centres including the Jagannath temple are located in the area covering the whole of Sankha Kshetra. Sankha or conch shell is one the Aiyudhas of Lord Vishnu, and it is for this reason that is the area covering the Sankha Kshetra is all the more important so far as the sacred character of the area is concerned. According to the *Utkal Khanda* of *Skandapurana* the Sankha Kshetra covers an area of 5 Kroshas (nearly 10 miles). Out of this area nearly half of it is submerged under water and the other half which lies above water is of the shape of a conch shell or Sankha. Since this part is most sacred it is called a Kshetra. Thus the name of this town has become Sankha Kshetra.

The belly part of Sankha Kshetra forms the western boundary. At the apical region lies the temple of Nilakantha near Indradymna tank. The naval part of the Sankha Kshetra is occupied by such sacred centres as Rohinikunda, Akshyabata, and the temple of Lord Jagannath. A deity called Ardhasini (Mausi Ma) is present in the middle part of the Sankha Kshetra. A hillock called Nilgiri is present in the Sankha Kshetra and it is this hill which has become the abode of the Lord Jagannath.

The Jagannath temple and the minor temples of minor deities and many other sacred places located within and outer compounds of the Jagannath temple form a sacred Zone. Similarly all the temples and shrines, tanks and many other categories of sacred places in and around *Sankha Kshetra* form another Zone. These two Zones taken together form a sacred Segment, which is divided into seven folds, which are discussed below:

The First Fold

The innermost or first fold which forms the naval or the Kshetra, is the seat of the divine platform on which the Lord Jagannath with his elder brother Balabhadra and their sister Subhadra, is installed.

The Second Fold

The second fold which is the outer layer of the first or the innermost fold, is hexagonal (*Satakonika*) in shape and in this are located four goddesses of power (*Chattusakti*), two tirthas, two sacred trees, *Garuda* (the vehicle of Lord Vishnu) and the top of the Nilagiri hill which is convex like the back of a tortoise. The goddesses are Bimala (the power of origin), Kamala (the power of desire), *Sarbamangala* (the power of knowledge) and Uttarai (the power of action). The sacred trees are Kalpapadapa (the roots striking deep into the earth) and *Salmalitaru* (the tree that fulfils desire). The tirthas are *Rohinikunda*, and *Pranitodakakunda* (otherwise called *Sunakuhan*-a well of gold).

The Third Fold

The third fold, which is the outer layer of the second fold, is the central part of the lotus-like structure having eight petals; each inlaid with an idol of Siva and a goddess. The eight Sivas are Agneswar, Bateswar, Khetrapaleswar, Chakreswar, Baikuntheswar, Pataleswar, Isaneswar, and Lokeswar. The eight goddesses are Dwarabasini, Mahabajreswari, Swanabhairabi, Bhadrakali,

Bhubaneswari, Mahakaliaghorea, Sitala, and Jagnyeswari. These deities are responsible for watching and guarding the first fold having the Supreme Lord at the centre of the Sacred Complex.

The Fourth Fold

The fourth fold, which is the outer coating of the third fold, forms the convex surface of the temple precinct (Mahakurma) and the inner compound wall.

The Fifth Fold

The fifth fold which is the outer layer of the fourth fold is the seat of the eight Sivas and eight goddesses. The Sivas are Bisweswar, Markandeswar, Mahakaleswar, Karnameswar, Mukteswar, Ugreswar, Kapilalochana, and Agreswar. The goddesses are Bisweswari, Saptamatrika, Dakhinakali, Charchika, Alameswari, Barahi, Banadurgeswari, and Basulikeswari. These deities are also in charge of watch and ward functions of the sacred complex.

The Sixth Fold

The sixth fold which is the outer layer of the fifth fold includes the noted five tirthas and the four original monastic seats of Ashrams. The five firthas are: (1) Manikarnika (A siva temple), (2) Swetaganga (a tank) (3) Indradyumna (the tank and the temple of Indradyumna, the mythic king of the golden age who miraculously received the logs of wood which were subsequently fashioned into images of Jagannath, Balabhadra and Subhadra and built the temple at Puri for their reception). (4) Markanda (the tank of Markandeya, hermitage of golden age and the temple of Markandeswar Siva whom the sage worshipped) and (5) Mahodadhi (the sea). The pilgrims visit these five tirthas while in Puri. It is the belief that the religious attainment that is obtained by going on a pilgrimage to the four important sacred centres of India-Gaya, Kasi, Hardwar, Prayag-is the same as the corresponding visit to the five tirthas located in the Puri pilgrim centre.

The four Ashrams, which are, located in the sixth fold of Sankha kshetra are Angirs in the east, Pandu in the west, Markandeya in the north, and Bhrigu in the south, These Ashrams were established in times beyond memory by the sages in Four Corners of the boundary of the Kshetra.

The Seventh Fold

The seventh fold, which is the outermost zone, consists of the sentries of the Sankha Kshetra and two pilgrim centres. The institutions, which the sentries guard, and the pilgrim centres are listed below:

Name of the deity	*Name of the place or institution guarded*
(1) Nilakantheswar (Siva)	Khetrapala(Governorof Kshetra).
(2) Narisingh	The place where Yajna (Fire worship) is performed
(3) Ardhasosani (Goddess)	Night watch woman.
(4) Bilweswar (Siva)	The apical region of the Sankha Kshetra
(5) Lokeswar (Siva)	The basal regin of the Sankha kshetra.
(6) Kapileswar (Siva)	The watchman of the Kshetra.
(7) Chakratirtha	The pilgrim centre of unique merits.
(8) Swargadwara	The passage to heaven (salvation)

The location of some temples like Baleswar and Jambeswar are much below the ground level, where as the Jagannath temple including the sacred centres which are found within the outer compound are present much above the ground level. The discussion about the location of the different sacred centres requires a study of the historical geography of the Sacred Geography of Puri town. Time and money are needed to take up this study and it is not possible to include this study and the present study on the Sacred Geography of Puri.

Annexure-I
Jagannath

Of all the regions on the earth', says an inspired sage in explaining the various places of pilgrimage of his pupils, 'India is the noblest; and of all the countries of India. Utkala boasts the highest renown. From end to end it is one vast region of pilgrimage. Its happy inhabitants live secure of a reception into the world of spirits; and even those who visit it, and bathe in its sacred rivers, obtain remission of their sins, though they may weigh like mountains. Who shall adequately describe its sacred streams, its temples, and its holy places, its fragrant flowers and exquisite fruits? Who shall estimate the soul's gain from a solourn in such a land ? But what need for enlarging on the praises of a realm, in which the gods themselves love to dwell?

Orissa is divided into four great regions of pilgrimage. From the moment the pilgrim passes the Baitarani River, on the high road forty miles north-east of Cuttack, he treads on holy ground. Behind him lies the secular world, with its cares for the things of this life; before him is the Promised Land, which he has been taught to regards a place of preparation for heaven. On the southern side of the river rises shrine after shrine to Siva, the All-Destroyer. On its very bank he beholds the house of Yama, the king of the dead; and as he crosses over, the priest whispers into his ear the last text which is breathed over the dying

Hindu at the moment the spirit takes it flight; 'In the dread gloom of Yama's halls is the tepid Baitarani River'. On leaving the stream he enters Jajpur, literally the City of Sacrifice, the headquarters of the region of pilgrimage, sacred to Parvati, the wife of the All-Destroyer. To the south-east is the region of pilgrimage sacred to the sun, now scarcely visited, with its matchless ruins looking down in desolate beauty across the Bay of Bengal. To the south-west is the region of pilgrimage dedicated to Siva, with its city of temples, which once clustered, according to native tradition, to the number of seven thousand, around the sacred lake. Beyond this, nearly due south, is the region of pilgrimage beloved of Vishnu, known to every hamlet throughout India, and to every civilised nation on earth, as the abode of Jagannath, the Lord of the World.

Extract from Temple of Puri by Asiatic Society

Annexure-II
An account of Sacred Characteristic of Puri

Of all places of Pilgrimage Shri Purusottam Kshetra is paramount place of pilgrimage. This Purusottam Kshetra is the destroyer of all ignorance and offers all results pity. This holy place is situated in the hillock known as Nilaparbata (Blue hill). This holy city is situated in a place in the seashore north of the sea and south of the Mahanadi. Extending in all directions from this place the Puri pilgrim centre has been most sacred and paramount pilgrim centre at every step. This pilgrim centre which extends from the seashore to the Nilgiri hills is the abode of all the objects of pity. Those having a pious heart and having bathe in Baitarani and having Darsan of Biraja goddess in Gada Kshetra (Jajapur) which is located on the bank of river Baitarani. These pious people who have darsan of Biraja goddess are eligible to have darsan of Ekamra Kanana, which is the city of temples of Siva. Those who have bathed in the tank of Bindusagar and having Darsan of Lord Lingaraj are fit to proceed to Konark for the darsan of Arka Kshetra, which is otherwise known as Padma Kshetra. Those who have bathed in Chandrabhaga River near Arka Kshetra are able to have Darsan of the bright Sun deity at that place. Those having done the abovementioned performances and become free from all evil characters are eligible to have Darsan of Shri Purusottam at Puri.

The blue hill which is endowed with all happiness having the shape of a conch shell extending over five crosas, has been the seat of all holy characters and those who have gone to this place have become free from all evil character and become holy in all respects. Those who have circumambulated the belly portion of Sankha Kshetra, which extends few places covering three crosas, have become free from all evil characters and endowed with all holly characters. The sea, which has touched the Shri Purusottam Kshetra, which is of three crosas in dimension, is recognized as famous Tirtha raja.

As the Purusottam Kshetra is divinely famous Kshetra and famous in all respects those who breathe their last at this place become free from all bondage of worldly activities. The Jamaraj is forbidden to take away those dead persons to his abode after their death. Even the incent who pass away at this place are free from the clutches of the Jamaraj. Even those who proceed on pilgrimage to this place and meet death enroute to Purosottam Kshetra are also free from the clutches of the Jamaraj.

Lord Bisweswar is present in the northern shore of the sea. This Sive deity destroys all powers of Jagannath and therefore Bisweswar becomes known as Jambeswar.

On the western, which is the apex, part of the Sankha Kshetra has been the abode of Nilakantha that means at the top of the Sankha Kshetra. On the western side lies the temple of Nilakantha. It is at this place extending upto one crosa has been the seat of Narayana. The belly portion of the conch shell is submerged under the sea since the sea touches the place where Narayana is sited this part of the sea is known as Tirtha Raja. Different deities are seated in different layers of the conch shell. In the second layer of the conch shell has been the abode of the Siva namely Kapalmochana. Likewise other layers have been the abode of many other deities, for example the third layer has been the place where Bimala is seated Shri Purusottam occupies the Naval region of Sankha Kshetra. Between the Shrine of Kopalamochana and the naval region of Sankha Kshetra the almighty Ardhasani is established. On the whole eight different Sivas and eight different Goddess are present in different layers of Sankha Kshetra.

The details of different layers and the sacred shrines and places present in such layers are given in Chapter-VI of the report.

Annexure-III
Sacred Places within the Jagannath Temple or Shrimandir

Plot No.	
1.	Ratnabedi
9, 9a	Jaya Bijaya Dwara
10.	Garuda Stamba (Pillar of Garuda deity)
11 a,b,c,	Bhoga Mandapa (Place where consecrated foods are kept)
26.	Baraha Mandir (the temple of Baraha)
37.	Radhakrishna Mandir (the temple of Radha Krishna)
41.	Pataleswar Mahadev (the temple of patales-war Siva)
43.	Shri Ramachandra Mandir (the temple of Lord Ramachandra)
45.	Konark Surya Thakura, Narayana mandir (the temple of Konark Sun deity Narayana)
48.	Nabagraha Mandir (the temple of Nabagraha)
54.	Laxmi Narayana Mandir (the temple of the Laxmi Narayana)

55.	Laxmi Mandir (the temple of Laxmi)
56.	Bedha Kali Mandir (the temple of Goddess Bedha Kali)
57.	Nilamadhaba Mandir (the temple of Nilamadhaba)
64.	Gopinath Mandir (the temple of Gopinath)
65.	Kanchi Ganesha Mandir (the temple Kanchi Ganesha)
66.	Sakhigopal Mandir (the temple of Sakhigopal)
72.	Shri Bimala Thakurani Mandir (the temple of Goddess Bimala)
74.	Chakranarayana Mandir, Bhadrinarayana Mandir (the temple of Chakranarayana and Bhadrinarayana)
78.	Rohini Kunda
79.	Kanchi Khari Ganesh or Natua Ganesh
81.	Nrushinha Mandir (the temple of Nrushinha)
82.	Muktimandap
83.	Mukteswar Mahadev (the Siva deity)
84.	Kshetrapala Mahadev (the Siva deity)
85.	Ananta Basudev Mahadev (the Siva deity)
86.	Kutam Chandi Mandir (the Goddess)
87.	Surya Mandir (Sun temple)
89.	Kalpabata

90.	Panchu Pandaba Mahadev (the Siva deity)
91.	Baraha Narayan Mandir (the temple of Baraha)
94.	Radha Krushna Mandir (the temple of Radha Krushna)
113.	Satyanarayana Mandir (the temple of Satyanarayana)
116.	Agniswara mandir (the temple of Agniswara)
118.	Brundabana Chandra Thakura Mandir (the temple Brundaban Chandra)
120.	Trertaya Dev. Shri Balabhadra, Subhadra and Jagannath temple

Outer Compound

136.	Ishaneswar Mahadev (the temple of Ishaneswar Siva)
137.	Dhabaleswar Mandir (the temple of Dhabaleswar Siva)
138-139	Parsunath or Kashinath Mahadev (the temple of Parsunath and Kashinath Siva)
148.	Snana Mandapa (Bathing Pedestal)
156.	Anandabazar
157.	Purbadwara (eastern gate)
157a.	Baisipahacha (22 steps)
159.	Patitapabana
160.	Sinhadwara (lion gate)
161, 162	Aruna Khamba

164. Kasi Biswanath Mandir (the temple of Kashibiswanath)

215. Mahadev Mandir (the temple of Mahadev Siva)

218. Shri Dakhineswar Mandir (the temple of Dakhineswar)

254. Durga Madhaba temple

156. Shri Sidheswar Mahadeba

257-258 The temple of Rameswar Mahadeba (Siva) including Four Dham Gokarneswar, Bhadrinath, Dwarikanath and Jagannath

269. Shri Dhabaleswar Mandir (the temple Shri Dhabaleswar (Siva)

276. Koili Baikuntha

Out Side the Temple

Narendra Tank

Markanda Tank

Swetaganga Tank

Samundra

Swargadwara

Chakratirtha

Indradyumna Tank

Lokanath temple

Gundicha Ghar

Glossary

Abakash	:	Morning offerings
Abatara	:	Evolution
Aiyudhas	:	Symbols
Akhada	:	A part of the street where gymnastic performances are performed
Akhanda Mekapa	:	A class of ritual functionaries
Ananda Bazar	:	The place where the consecrated foods are sold
Ananda Nata	:	A kind of dance
Anka	:	Ancient manner in which different years are counted.
Aruna Sthamba	:	Sun pillar
Asokastami	:	A kind of festival
Aswadwara	:	Horse gate
Athuranulla ghat	:	18 passage of the bridge called Athuranulla
Bachanika	:	Narrations
Badadanda	:	Grand road
Badasinghara	:	Last offering at night
Baishnavas	:	Ascetics
Baisipahacha	:	Twenty two steps
Baitarani	:	A river
Balukhanda	:	A section of Puri town
Basanda	:	Boycott

Batis	A kind of measurement of land
Batpeadas	Road peon
Beharan dwar	The door of the place where the functionaries are seated
Beharan Mandap	A platform used for sitting by the officials/functionaries of the temple
Bethia	Labourers
Bhanand house	a room used for festivities
Bhandari	Barber
Bhanga	Narcotic
Bhendia	A strong and stout young man
Bhogamandapa	Place where consecrated foods are placed
Bhurrunga Jatree	A kind of pilgrim
Bidyapati	Minister of Indradyumna
Bindusagar	A sacred tank at Bhubaneswar
Biswabasu	A sabar who was worshiping Lord Jagannath
Brahmacharies	Calibrates
Brahmapuras	One kind of sasan village
Caukis	Stations or centers
Chaitra	Month of May
Chakrabula Ekadasi	Eleventh day of a month on which fasting is observe
Chatra Bhoga	Public food
Chaturdasi	14th day
Chera Panhara	sweeping the three cars with a golden broom
Chhatisa Nijoga	36 sebaks in orders
Daitabana	A typical part of the forest
Daiva tirthas	One category of pilgrim center

Dakhina	: Fees of gift given to a priest for his ritual performance
Dantapura	: particular place of Puri
Darshan	: Seeing
Daru	: wood
Dasabatara	: Evolutionary stages
Dasanami	: A class of sect.
Dasara	: A festival
Debarchan	: Worshiping god
Deepa	: Lamps
Desees	: Local pilgrim
Deswari	: Country side
Deula	: Temple
Devadasis	: Female sebakas of the deities. Mainly they perform singing and dancing before the deities to invoke slumber
Dham	: A pilgrim center
Dharmasala	: Inn where pilgrims are lodged
Dharmasastras	: Religious literatures
Diarist	: Despatching clerk
Dustak	: Passport
Dwipa	: Island
Ekharajat mahal	: A territory having land of the temple.
Ghatua	: Pilgrim touts
Gikha	: A caste
Gopies	: decibels
Gumasta	: Assistant
Gundicha ghar	: The temple where the deities are placed for 9 days during car festival

Haṇdi kudia	:	Earthen vessels
Hastidwara	:	Elephant gate
Jagamohan	:	A particular place in the temple
Jagir	:	Service land
Jamnika Kshetra	:	Puri
Janma	:	Birth
Janmasiddhi	:	Birth celebration
Jatrees	:	Pilgrims
Jatri Gumasta	:	Assistants of Panda who take care of the pilgrims
Jatri Panda	:	Pandas in charge of pilgrims
Jegaghar	:	Gymnastic house
Kaliadalana Ekadasi	:	A type of festival
Kalpa	:	A special name for a hold object
Kangals	:	destitute
Kapila Sanhita	:	A sacred text
Karachali	:	Pay tax
Karmani	:	Service record
Khanjahs	:	donation of gifts
Khasmahal	:	A part of region in Puri town
Khei	:	Payment to a functionary in the form of consecrated foods.
Kotha Khanja	:	Royal gift for share
Kunda	:	A mini tank
Kuruma bedha	:	inner compound
Madala Panji	:	Almanac in which the activities relating to the temple are mentioned
Madhyana Dupa	:	Mid day offering
Mahabedi	:	The great platform
Mahaprasada	:	Consecrated food
Malikana	:	Share

Mandapa	:	Platform
Mandirmala	:	The city of temple
Math	:	Monastery
Meda	:	A part of the car
Meghanada Prachira	:	Outer wall of the Jagannath temple
Mohadadhi	:	The sea
Muktimandap	:	Pavilion of Brahmin Pandits
Murdhani	:	1st fold the Sankha Kshetra.
Natamandap	:	dancing hall
Nijogas	:	An organization of ritual functionaries
Nilachala	:	Where Lord Jagannath is situated
Nilakandar	:	A part of hillock
Nirmalya	:	Rice grains half cooked in the temple kitchen
Nitis	:	Daily round of worship
Pagoda	:	Name of place
Pakhaja	:	Drum
Panchami	:	Fifth day
Panicky	:	Cutting instrument
Panthi	:	The manner in which the food offered
Parichha	:	A class of sebaka
Patitapabana	:	Lord Jagannath
Pothis	:	Ancient books
Pratiharis	:	A class of sebaka
Purana	:	Hymn
Purnima	:	Full moon day
Purusa Mandap	:	Name of the palace
Rasalila	:	A performance
Rath	:	Car

Rishi	:	A saint
Sabaradipaka	:	Name of a place
Sahi	:	Street
Sahijatra	:	Street festival
Sambhu	:	Lord Siva
Sanga	:	Comrades
Sanyasi	:	Saint
Saradhabali	:	A part of the Puri.
Sastra	:	Religious script
Sataisa	:	Twenty seven
Seba basanda	:	Boycott from service
Sebapuja	:	Service
Singhadwara	:	Lion's gate
Sinhasana	:	Throne
Srinahara	:	King's palace
Swargadwara	:	Gateway of heaven
Tirthayatra	:	Pilgrimage visit
Topabana	:	Name of a place

Bibliography

Nirmal Kumar Bose Life, Works and Vision, Nityananda Patnaik, Edited by Tulika Sen, Published by the Asiatic Society, Park Street Kolkata-6, April-2003.

Jagannath in Alien Eyes, N. P. Tripathy, etc., Published by Utkal Cultural Wing of Shri Jagannath Seva Samiti, Kolkata, 2003.

The Orissa Gazette, May 7, 1955, Works by L. Panda, Special Officer in charge of Shri Jagannath Temple, Government Press Cuttack.

Kashi Myth and Reality of a Classical Cultural Tradition, B. N. Saraswati, Published by the Registrar, Indian Institute of Advanced Study, Simla 171005, and printed by Universal Advertisers (Printing Division), New Delhi-110055, 1975.

Puri A Gazetteer, L.S.S.O. Malley, Published by Usha Publications, 1984.

Anthropological Studies on Indian Societies, Nityananda Patnaik, Published by the Modern Book Depot, Bhubaneswar-1, Orissa, 2001.

Niladri Mohadaya, Vol.1 by Dr. Braja Kishore Swain, Published at Jagannath Process, Cuttack, 2000.

Cultural Tradition in Puri, N. Patnaik, Published by Indian Institute of Advance Study, Simla, Printed at Dhawan Printing Works, Mayapuri, New Delhi-110064, 1977.

Sacred Complex of Orissa, Dr. Nityananda Patnaik, Published by Gyan Publishing House, New Delhi-110002, 2000.

The Sacred Complex of Kashi, A Microcosm of Indian Civilization, By L. P. Vidyarthi, etc., Published by Naurang Rai, Concept Publishing Company, New Delhi 110035, 1979.

The Sacred Complex in Hindu Gaya, L. P. Vidyarthi, Published by Concept Publishing Company, Delhi-110035, 1961.

Madala Panji, Mrutyunjay Nayak, Published by Friends Publishers, Cuttack-753002, Orissa (India), and Second Enlarged Edition: 1997.

Skanda Purana Utkal Khanda, Pandit Shri Harihara Mishra, Published by Dharma Grantha Store, Cuttack-2, 2001.

The Cult of Jagannath and the Regional Tradition of Orissa, Anncharlott Eschmann, etc., Published by Monohar Publications, New Delhi-110002, 1978.

Puri Lord Jagannath's Dhaam, Subhadra Sen Gupta, Published by Rupa & Co., New Delhi 110 002, Printed by Rekha Printers Pvt. Ltd., 2002.

Badrinath and Kedarnath, The Dhaams in the Himalayas, Subhadra Sen Gupta, Rupa & Co., New Delhi 110 002, Printed by Rekha Printers Pvt. Ltd., 2002.

Lord Jagannath His Temple, Cult and Festivals, Himanshu S. Patnaik, Published by Aryan Books International, New Delhi-110002, Year 1994

Sri Purusottam Kshetra's Prachinata and Mandir Pratista, Dr. Satyanarayana Rajgur July 1996, Rath Yatra Special of Utkal Prasanga.

Index

R

S